Introduction

At one time or another, everyone has encountered a hand-carved, flat-plane style sea captain figurine. The beautiful simplicity that the flat-plane style brings to the character has made these pieces a staple of the tourist trade, while the classic subject matter and the speed at which they can be carved have made the sea captain a favorite of woodcarvers. For my interpretation of this classic character, I wanted to create a sea captain with natural balance and a relaxed pose that incorporated all of the realistic details that I like to put into my carvings.

The Design Process

If you plan to carve realistic figures, I cannot stress enough the importance of being a constant student of human anatomy. A good understanding of the structures of the human body will save you a great deal of frustration in both the design and carving processes. When planning a carving of a human figure, the first tool I start with is my anatomy book. It's also the last tool I put away, as I reference it often while carving.

The second tool I use is clay, so I can construct a model of the figure I have in mind. Creating a clay model allows you to work out all the details of the carving, from pose to posture to features, before you cut your piece of wood. Working in clay before carving doesn't save any time, but it does allow you to ensure anatomy and proportions are correct so your end result is a better carving.

The Carving Process

My carving process involves blocking out a carving into a series of planes. First I create large planes; then, as I refine each of these areas, I slowly break them down into smaller planes. I start from the top, at the front of my carving, and work my way down and around to the back. I repeat this process as many imes as it takes to complete the carving.

Typically my carvings will go through four stages: blocking out the planes, roughing in the shapes, refining the forms, and adding the final details. Although it's often hard to tell where one stage ends and another begins, it's important to work the carving as a whole and not progress too far ahead in one area. This allows you to make subtle tweaks to your whole piece as it takes shape.

And finally, remember to refer to your reference materials. They're some of the best tools you have.

Materials & Tools

MATERIALS:

- Basswood, 3¼" (8.3cm) thick: 6" x 12¼" (15.2cm x 31.1cm)
- Basswood, 1¼" (3.2cm) thick: short post, 1⅝" x 2⅝" (4.1cm x 6.7cm); medium post, 2¼" x 4¼" (5.7cm x 10.8cm)
- Sandpaper: 320 grit
- Cyanoacrylate (CA) glue
- Sealer, such as Bullseye Sealcoat
- Acrylic paints: ivory black, titanium white, unbleached titanium, burnt umber, burnt sienna, vermilion, ultramarine blue, cerulean blue, gray

TOOLS:

- Band saw
- Carving knives: assorted shapes and sizes
- Straight chisel: 5/16" (8mm)
- Skew chisel: 5/16" (8mm)
- Spoon-bent skew chisels: 1/16" (2mm) right, 1/16" (2mm) left
- #2 gouges: ½" (13mm), 1" (25mm)
- #5 gouges: ⅛" (3mm), 5/16" (8mm), ½" (or 12mm), 1" (25mm)
- #5 palm gouge: ⅛" (3mm)
- #7 gouge: 5/32" (4mm)
- #9 gouges: 3/16" (5mm), ¾" (19mm)
- #11 gouges: 1/32" (1mm), ⅛" (3mm), ¼" (6mm), ½" (13mm)
- V-tools, 60°: 1/16" (2mm), ⅛" (3mm), ¼" (6mm)
- Drill with bits: 1/16" (2mm), ⅛" (3mm), 3/16" (5mm), 5/16" (8mm)
- Mallet
- Gel pens: black, red, purple
- Paintbrushes
- Toothpicks

Cleaning Tools:

- Dental picks
- Diamond rifflers
- Sanding sticks
- Rotary tool with small bit (optional)

Measuring Tools:

- Ruler
- Dividers
- Calipers
- Contour/profile gauge

The author used these products for the project. Substitute your choice of brands, tools, and materials as desired.

Full-size patterns are on pages 28-31.

Blocking Out the Planes

1

Transfer the front- and side-view patterns to the wood. Using a band saw, remove excess wood from the front and side profiles of the transferred pattern. *Due to the size of the starting block, the two smaller posts were added to the carving later.* Using a ¾" (19mm) #9 gouge and a 1" (25mm) #2 gouge, remove the major areas of waste wood. Start by carving across the front of the body, leaving a block for the left hand; from the front of the post, stop-cutting underneath the left hand; in front of the right leg and ankle, between the left shin and the top of the right foot; and in front of the right and left arms from the top of the forearm up to the shoulder (creating the crook of the elbow).

TIP

USE A CARVING STAND

I'm a workbench carver. I prefer to have my project secured to a table or carving stand while in progress. This not only makes carving far safer, but also easier since both hands are free for strength and control, or to use the mallet.

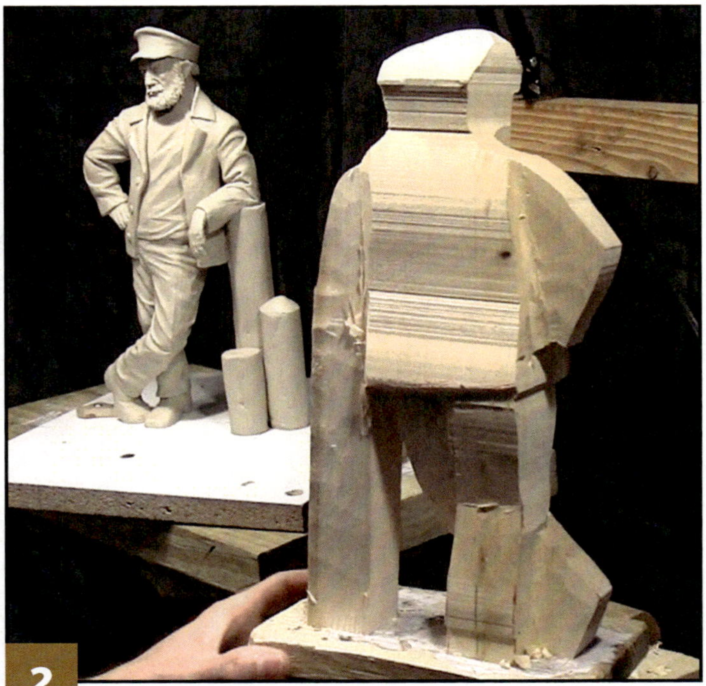

2

Remove the excess wood from the back. Start with the wood behind the post. Then, remove the excess wood behind the left foot, knee, and lower leg. Remove wood from behind the arms, so they are no longer in line with the back of the coat. Be careful not to make the shoulders too thin. Then, create a plane that angles from the heel of the left foot down the side of the left shoe to the toe of the right shoe.

3

Turn the head slightly to give this carving a dynamic pose. To do this, draw a centerline, starting on the face and continuing over top of the head and down to neck level. At the level of the nose, make a mark $\frac{3}{16}$" (5mm) to the left of the centerline. Make a mark $\frac{3}{16}$" (5mm) to the right of the centerline on the back of the head. Draw a new centerline using these points; I use a contour or profile gauge. Use the new line as the centerline for the head; disregard the original line.

BLOCKING OUT THE PLANES

4 **Mark the bottom and the bridge of the nose.** The bottom of the nose will be 10½" (26.7cm) from the ground the carving is standing on (bottom of his feet). Measure ½" (1.3cm) upward from the bottom of the nose and mark the location for the brow. On the centerline, at the bottom of the nose and the bridge, make ⅛" (3mm)-deep horizontal stop cuts. To create the angle of the ridge of the nose and the plane of the mouth area, carve to each of the stop cuts using a 1" (25mm) gauge. Make sure that these planes are perpendicular to the centerline of the head, as this is what creates the subtle turn of the head.

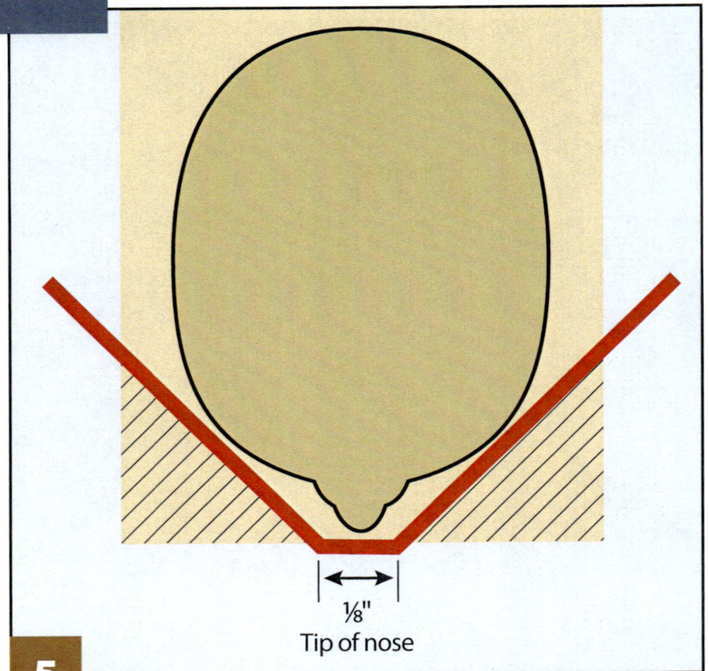

5 **Mark a ⅛" (3mm) width for the tip of the nose.** Starting at those points on both sides of the nose, use a 1" (25mm) #5 gouge to carve planes at a 45° angle from the tip of the nose toward the ears. This creates the 90° angle of the face. Avoid cutting into the brim of the hat. The plane of the ridge of the nose should be triangular in shape, flaring out to the width of the brow. Using the #5 gouge allows this plane to curve out at the jawline, leaving extra wood for the beard.

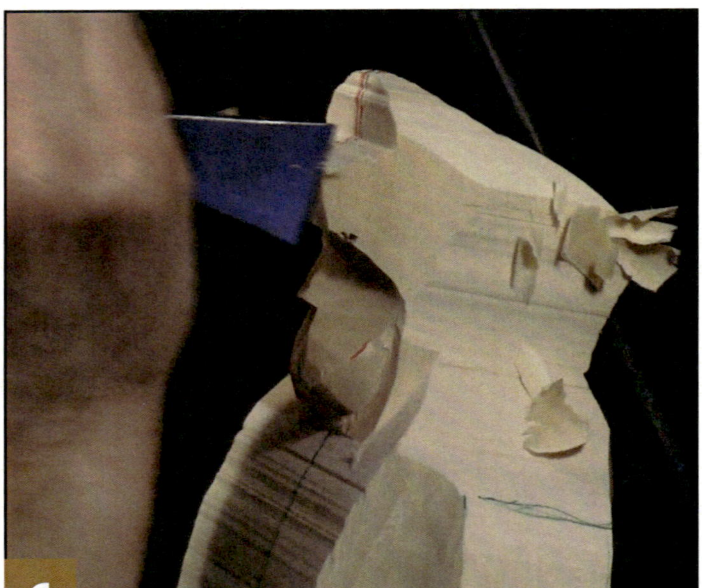

6 **Make a stop cut along the edge of the beard.** Use the 1" (25mm) #5 gouge. Square off the end of the hat brim to make it perpendicular to the centerline of the head. Mark the total width of the head and hat at 1¾" (4.4cm). Carve the head down to this width with the 1" (25mm) #2 gouge. Make the planes on the sides of the head parallel to the centerline. Use a ½" (13mm) #11 gouge to carve the front of the hat above the brim and make it perpendicular to the centerline.

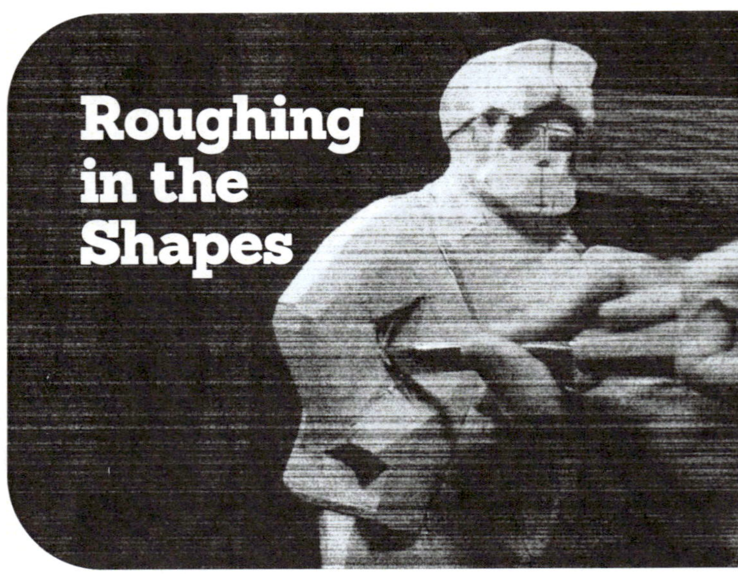

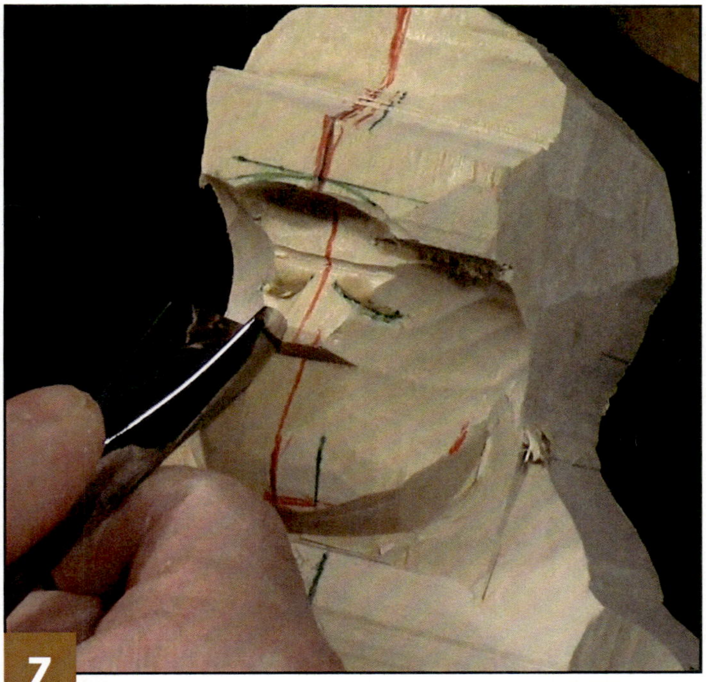

7 **Measure up 3⁄8" (1cm) from the bottom of the nose on both sides to mark the inner corners of the eyes, be sure to leave some width for the bridge of the nose.** Draw arches starting at these marks, following the bottom edge of the eye orbits where the bags and wrinkles are located. Stop-cut along these lines with a 5⁄16" (8mm) #5 gouge. Starting from below the nose, carve alongside both sides of the nose with the 3⁄4" (19mm) #9 gouge up to the stop cuts. This forms the shape of the nose.

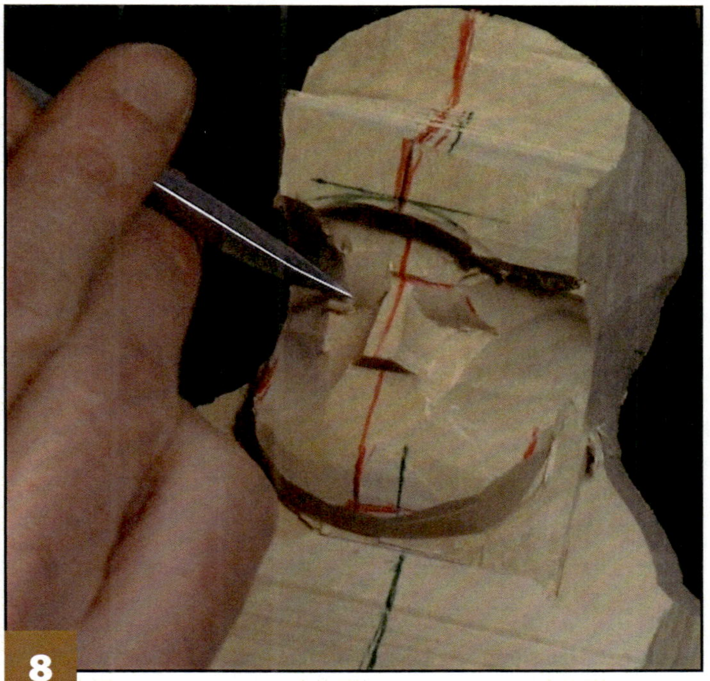

8 **Carve from the brow at an angle to the bottom of the stop cuts to create the slope of the eye mound.** You can make this cut two ways: by carving from the brow down to the stop cut with a knife, or by cutting in from the side with the 5⁄16" (8mm) #5 gouge so that it creates an angled plane from the brow to the bottom of the stop cut.

9 **Narrow the width of the hat brim to its final size.** Refer to the pattern. Draw the bottom edge of the hat and mark the ears. Mark the 13⁄16" (3cm) width of the face, and mark the location of the sideburns on the side. Narrow the face down by carving it back to the front edge of the sideburns with the 3⁄4" (19mm) #9 gouge. Use a 1⁄8" (3mm) #11 gouge and the 5⁄16" (8mm) #5 gouge to narrow the temple area under the edge of the hat.

10 **Draw the location of the lapels and the edges of the coat.** Define the edges of the coat with a 1⁄4" (6mm) V-tool. Use the 1" (25mm) #5 gouge to remove the wood between the edges of the coat. Angle the right edge of the coat from the lapel to the bottom corner so the bottom corner of the coat protrudes 1⁄8" (3mm) from the front of the right leg.

ROUGHING IN THE SHAPES

11 **Cut the shoulders down to size were the sleeves join the shoulders.** Carve with the 1" (25mm) #2 gouge from the back of the sleeve into the middle of the back to create angled planes where the shoulder blades would be. These planes should extend about 1½" (3.8cm) toward the center of the back. Use the ¼" (6mm) V-tool to stop-cut the outside edge of the lapel, and then thin the front of the shoulders. Use the 1" (25mm) #5 gouge to carve the front of the right shoulder. Use a ½" (13mm) #2 gouge to carve between the left forearm and lapel and to carve the angle on the coat from the edge back to the shoulder.

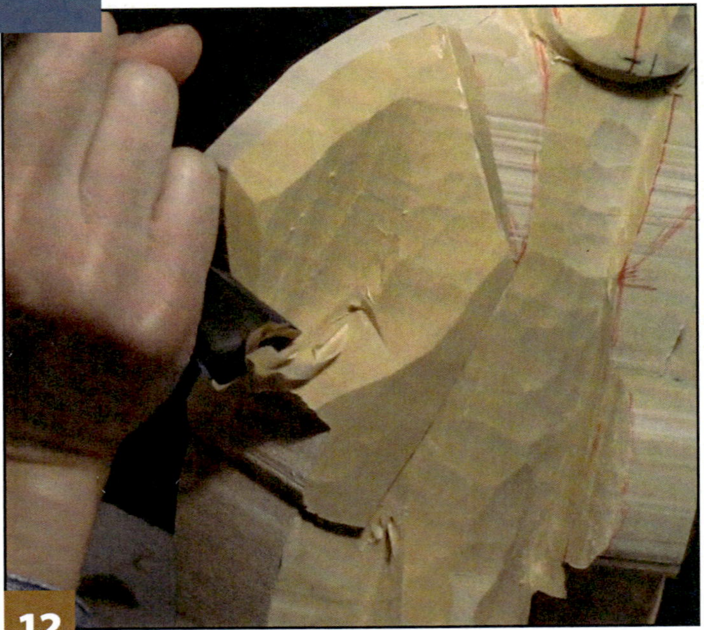

12 **Carve the corners of the upper arm off at a 45° angle.** This will leave a ½" (1.3cm)-wide flat area in the center of the sides of the arms. The end of the right sleeve will be more diamond shaped in the cross section, so it will need to be tapered more to the centerline of the side of the arm.

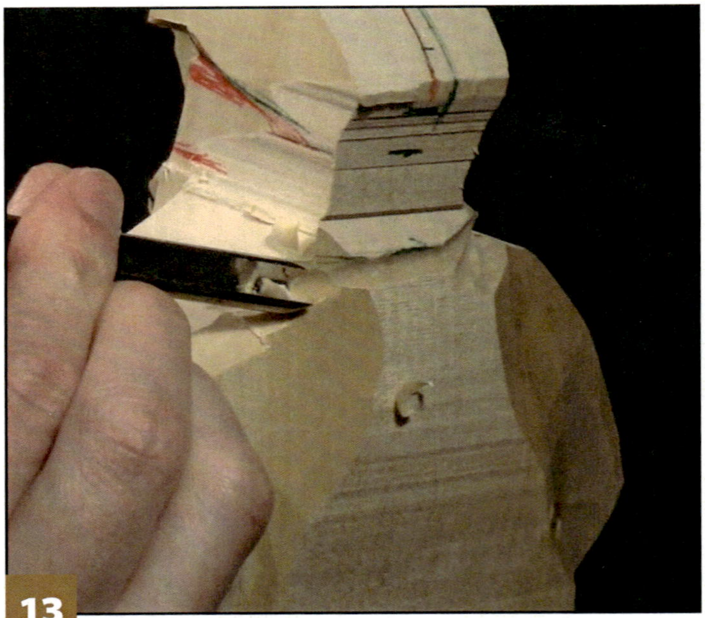

13 **Draw the edge of the collar across the back of the shoulders.** Make a soft stop cut (for the time being), along this line with a ¼" (6mm) #11 gouge. Then, rough in the shape of the collar with the ¾" (19mm) #9 gouge and the ½" (13mm) #2 gouge. Then, farther define the soft stop cut of the edge of the collar with the ⅛" (3mm) #11 gouge.

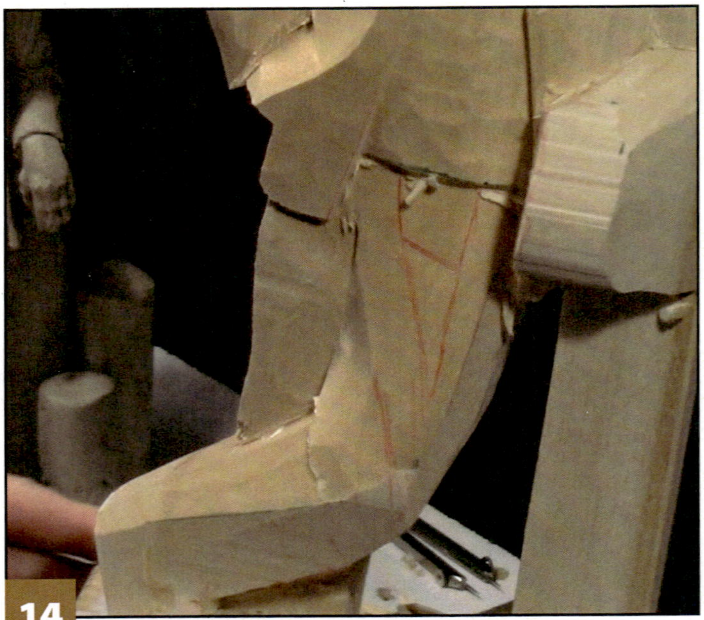

14 **Make a soft stop cut at the bottom edge of the shirt.** Use the ⅛" (3mm) #11 gouge. Carve a plane from the left knee to the crotch with the 1" (25mm) #5 gouge. Knock the outside corner of the left leg off with the 1" (25mm) #2 gouge from where the crease runs down the center of the leg to about the middle of the thigh on the side. From where the crease fades out at the level of the crotch, there is a flat plane that goes straight up to the bottom of the shirt.

15 **Draw centerlines on all sides of the legs.** Carve the planes around the ankle of the right leg. Make them come to a point on the centerlines of the back and sides. Use the 1" (25mm) #5 gouge to create three planes running from the middle of the thigh to the back of the knee. This will begin to separate the back of the thigh from the buttock and will establish the major folds in that area. Remove ¼" (6mm) from the front right corner of the right thigh. Trim the sole of the left shoe so it's perpendicular to the line of the lower left leg.

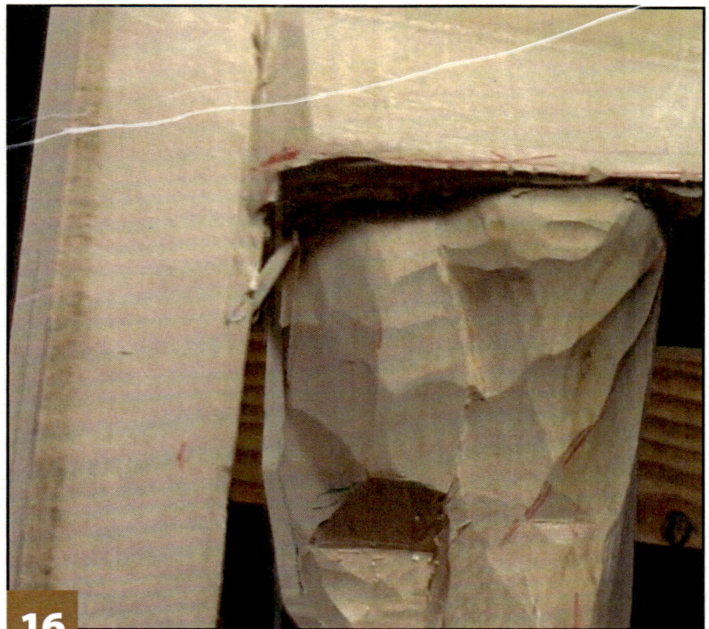

16 **Create a plane on the back left corner of the left leg from the bottom edge of the coat to the knee.** Make this plane at a 45° angle compared to the planes of the block of wood. It starts at the centerline of the back of the left leg. Use the ¼" (6mm) #11 gouge to stop-cut below the bottom edge of the coat, and then use the 1" (25mm) #2 gouge to create this plane. There is a large triangular fold in the pants that juts out from the back of the left knee. The point of this fold is 3⅛" (7.9cm) off the ground. Carving this plane allows you to get the top of the left calf thinned down to size, which is 1¼" (3.2cm) measured from the front of the left knee. It will look like you took a notch out of the back of the leg.

17 **Make two cuts to begin separating the legs.** Use the 1" (25mm) #5 gouge. Start the first cut at the peak of the triangular fold behind the left knee. Continue to angle toward the crotch with the second cut as you carve between the legs.

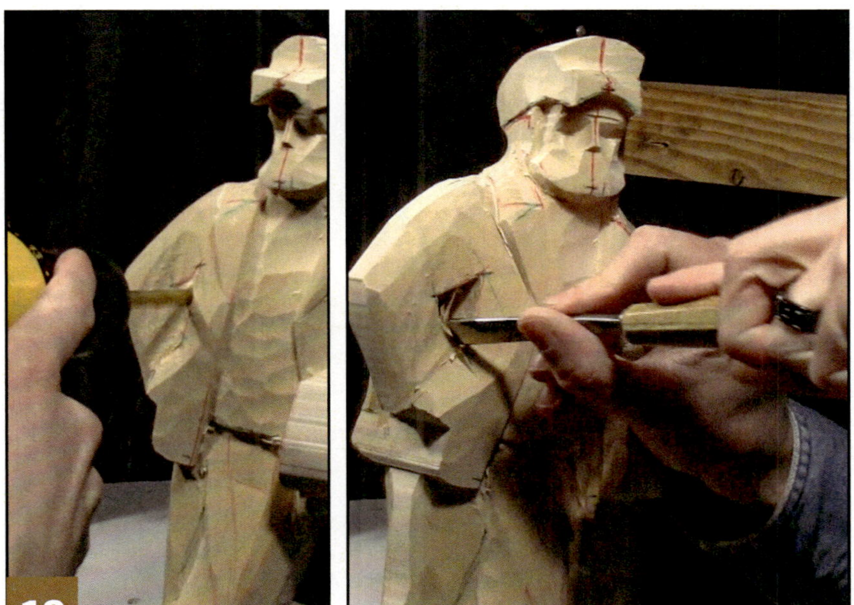

18 **Mark the wood to remove between each arm and the body.** Drill through the area under the right arm with a 5⁄16" (8mm)-diameter bit. Drill two ⅛" (3mm)-diameter holes (one right above the other) under the left arm. Use the ⅛" (3mm) #11 gouge, a ½" (13mm) #2 gouge, and a 5⁄16" (8mm) skew chisel to finish piercing under the right arm. Make sure that you carve straight through; do not cut into the body by accident.

ROUGHING IN THE SHAPES

19 **Make a stop cut under the right hand and sleeve cuff.** Use the ¼" (6mm) #11 gouge. Use your choice of #2 gouge to wrap the coat around the body from below the hand to the bottom edge of the coat by creating five planes that mimic the shape of the leg and hip. Leave the coat above the depth of the leg and hip. Measure and mark the top edge of the right hand. Create a flat plane for the back of the right hand and fingers by carving with the 1" (25mm) #2 gouge from the pinky finger side of the hand into the body until you have a ¾" (1.9cm)-wide space for the back of the hand. Then, use the ¼" (6mm) V-tool to separate the end of the fingers from the coat.

20 **Draw the seam where the right sleeve meets the shoulder.** The sleeve should be 1¼" (3.2cm) thick from front to back. After carving it to that thickness, use the ¼" (6mm) #11 gouge to carve into the armpit from the front starting about ½" (1.3cm) above the armpit where the bottom of the sleeve meets the body. On the back, start ¼" (6mm) above the armpit as you carve in toward the center of the bottom side of the sleeve. This will allow you to start rounding the body into the opening under the right arm and create planes to round the bottom of the upper arm. Round the corners of the lower arm into the separation between the arm and the body.

21 **Measure 7" (17.8cm) above the ground to mark the end of the right thumb.** Holding a ruler straight across the back, mark 1¼" (3.2cm) in from the bottom corner of the right cuff. Mark 1½" (3.8cm) from the tip of the fingers. These three marks may not appear to come together until you have gotten the thumb roughed in. Use the ½" (13mm) #2 gouge to cut the top edge of the thumb, which is a level plane. Then, carve the plane of the back of the thumb (the side with the thumbnail) so it angles from where the end touches the coat to where it disappears into the sleeve. Use the ¼" (6mm) #11 gouge to remove the waste wood below the thumb and the end of the sleeve. As you carve across under the thumb and the sleeve, angle the cuts down so that you leave plenty of wood for the palm of the hand under the sleeve.

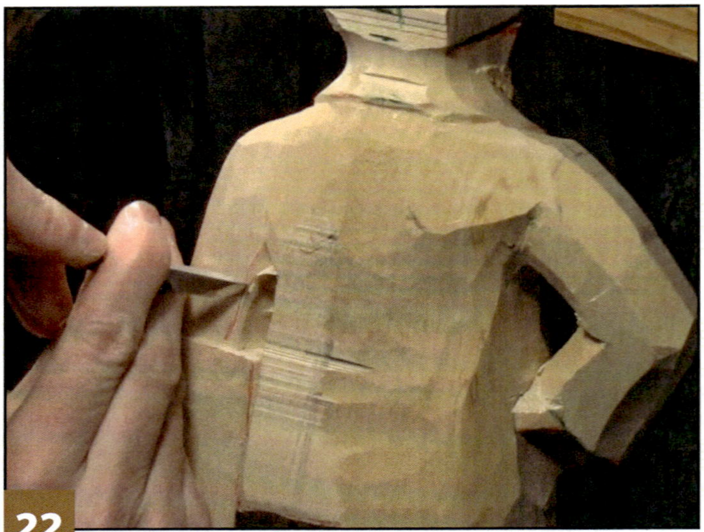

22 **Draw the top of the post and the planes around the back of the left armpit.** Use the skew chisel or a carving knife to carve the planes around the armpit between the arm and the body. These cuts remind me of chip carving, as you'll basically be taking out a triangular-shaped chip from between the arm and body. While you're working in this area, stop-cut the top of the post and adjust the planes of the back of the left arm so the elbow is inside of the edge of the post by ⅛" (3mm).

23 **Refine the planes of the shoulder blades and create the planes of the back of the coat.** Use the 1" (25mm) #5 gouge and the 1" (25mm) #2 gouge. Use the 1" (25mm) #5 gouge to create the depression between the shoulder blades and to help wrap the planes of the coat around the body at the waist. Make a stop cut down the side of the post so the planes of the coat can be tucked around inside of the edge of the post.

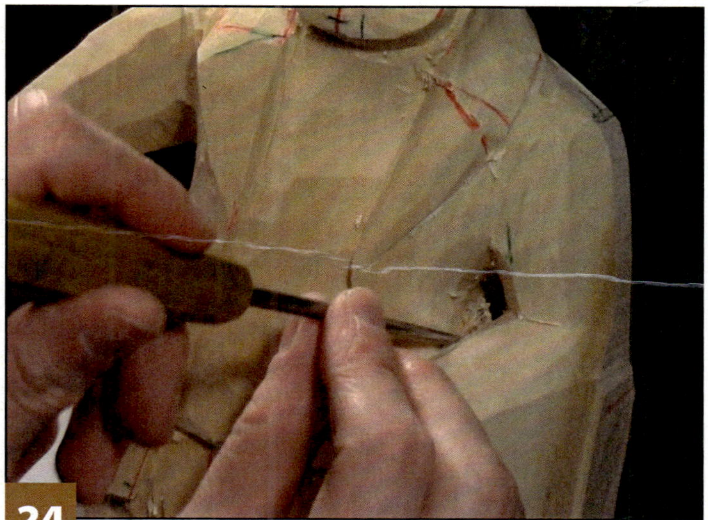

24 **Finish piercing between the body and left arm.** Work the front of the armpit similar to the way you shaped the back in Step 21. Measure and mark out the shapes of the planes before cutting. Use the 5⁄16" (8mm) skew chisel, a 1⁄8" (3mm) #5 gouge, and the carving knives to finish piercing between the left arm and the body. As you clean and shape the hole, do not make the width of the opening any bigger than necessary or you risk carving into the body or arm. Thin the left shoulder down to 1¼" (3.2cm) wide from front to back where the sleeve meets the body. Then, adjust the planes of the coat with the ½" (13mm) #2 gouge so that they flow from the edge of the left lapel to the armpit and from the collar to the shoulder.

Carving Smooth, Convex Surfaces

Using a gouge can help you carve smooth round surfaces. Turn the tool over so the inside is against the wood. The curvature of the tool will create the outside surface of any round object. If your tool isn't the right curvature, though, it's always better to use a flatter one so the corners don't dig into the wood. Also, never underestimate the skew chisel's ability to create rounded surfaces. It'll take a lot of little cuts, but you can smooth a rounded surface really nicely with a skew chisel.

25 **Mark and stop-cut the end of the left sleeve.** Use the ¼" (6mm) V-tool. Make sure the mark and cut are perpendicular to the line of the forearm. Establish the plane of the back of the left hand by carving at an angle up to the end of the sleeve with the 1" (25mm) #2 gouge. Mark ¾" (1.9cm) from the end of the left sleeve, where the left wrist is, along this plane. That is the location of the knuckles of the left hand, and the hand should be ¾" (1.9cm) wide at that point. The line of the knuckles should be perpendicular to the direction of the arm. From the line of the knuckles, carve a plane for the fingers straight down. Then, mark ¾" (1.9cm) from the knuckles to find the tips of the fingers. Trim off anything that is hanging down past the tips of the fingers, but leave wood for the bottom edge of the coat behind the hand.

26 **Remove ⅝" (1.6cm) of wood from under the left forearm.** Everything that is in front of the end of the left sleeve should be left hanging down so that you'll have extra wood for the inside of the fingers. Use the ¼" (6mm) #11 gouge to quickly remove the majority of the wood, and then clean up the corners with the ½" (13mm) #2 gouge. If there is any extra wood outside of the pinky side of the left hand, remove it now. Angle the plane of the outside edge of the left sleeve under the arm by about $^{3}/_{16}$" (5mm) with the ½" (13mm) #2 gouge.

27 **Draw a centerline down each side of the post.** Then, draw another line between the edge of the post and the centerline on each side to divide the post into four equal vertical sections. Make a mark 1⅞" (4.8cm) from the bottom for the ropes. Then, carve between the lines with the ½" (13mm) #2 gouge to transform the square into an octagon.

Interpreting Photos

I talk a lot about the planes of the body and clothing in this project, and it's often very difficult to determine where the major planes of a carving should be based on photos. One trick to help with that is to remember that while you're roughing out the shape of your carving, there is almost always a flat plane from the ridge (or high point) of one clothing wrinkle to the next.

Refining the Forms

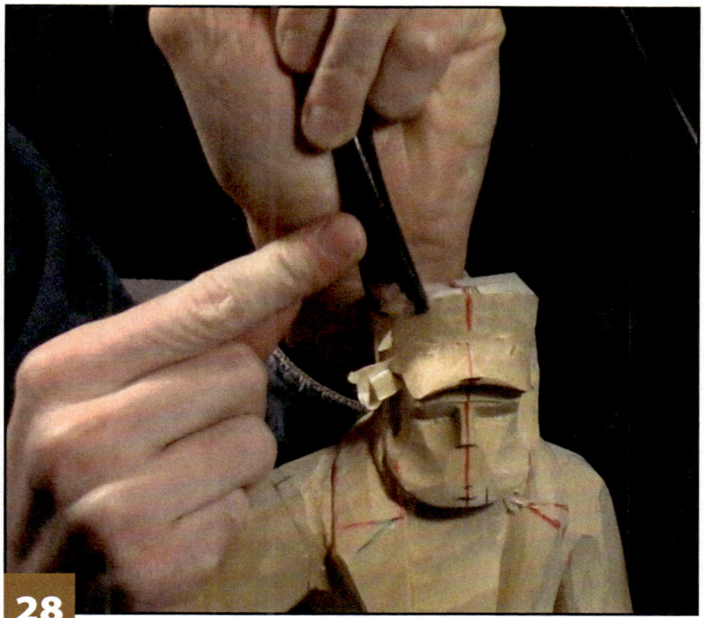

28 **Thin the hat bill down to just under 1⅜" (3.5cm) wide.** Use the 5⁄16" (8mm) #5 gouge. Use the 1" (25mm) #5 gouge to create the curvature of the bottom side of the bill. Use the same gouge to rough out the top of the bill, but use the ½" (13mm) #2 gouge upside down to finish creating the curve on the top of the bill. Draw the shape of the top of the hat, and then round the front of the hat with the 1" (25mm) #5 gouge.

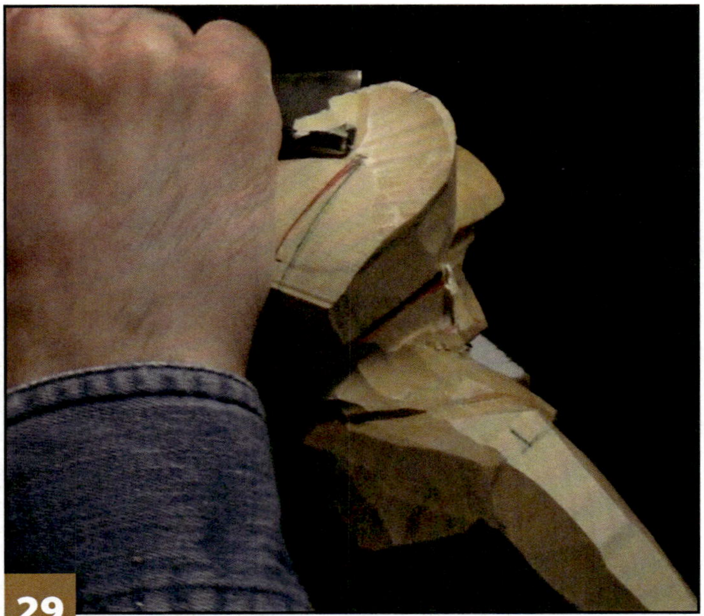

29 **Draw the top edge of the hat as it wraps around the head.** Start above where the ear would be with a 1" (25mm) #5 gouge and carve across to the line at the top of the head to add a shallow depression to the edge and crown of the hat. Because we have not set the location of the back of the head yet (thus giving the flexibility to carve the face deeper if needed), only do the front half of the hat for now.

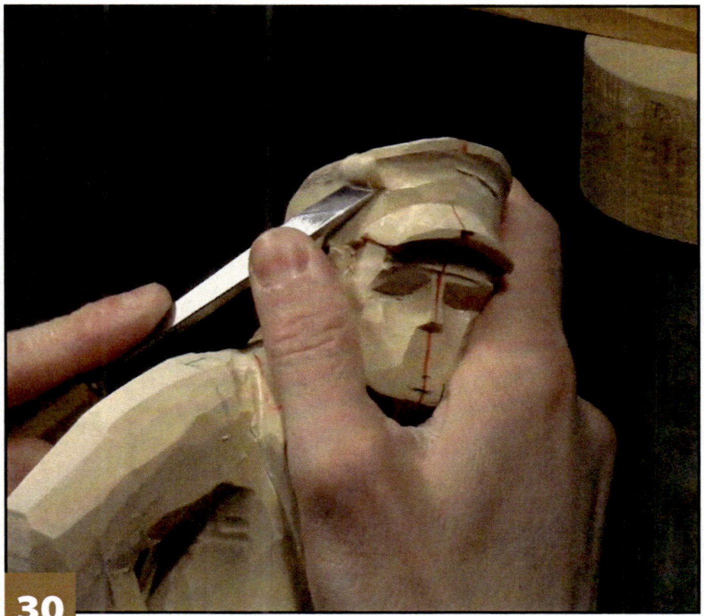

30 **To accentuate the top edge of the front of the hat, carve a groove around the front of the hat with the ¼" (6mm) #11 gouge.** The center of the groove should be ⅛" (3mm) deep and ¼" (6mm) down from the top edge, but the groove depth decreases to nothing on the sides of the hat. Blend and round the edge of this groove to the edge of the hat. Then, carve at an angle from the base of the bill to the bottom of the groove with a skew chisel or knife. Round the top front edge of the hat with the 5⁄16" (8mm) #5 gouge used upside down.

REFINING THE FORMS

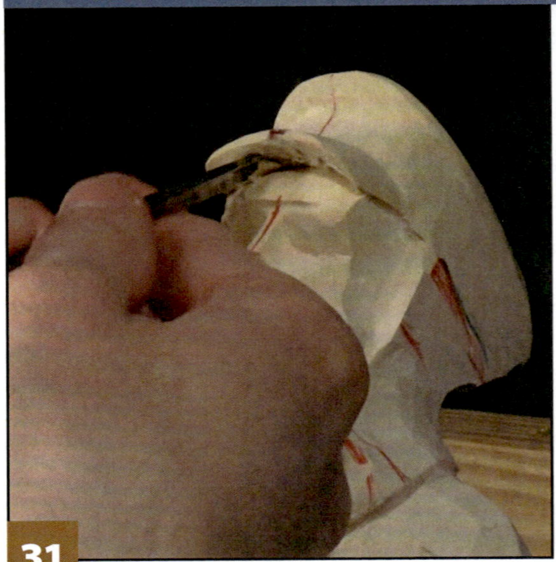

31 **Make a stop cut under the hat bill.** Use the 5⁄16" (8mm) #5 gouge. Angle the forehead back to fit under the hat by carving up to the stop cut with the ½" (13mm) #2 gouge. Use a knife to carve the forehead to its final depth. You will probably have to push the brow farther into the face and adjust the angle of the nose in order to keep the forehead from being too sloped, but that can be determined better after you have done the eyes. Allow the hat bill to become thicker as you go deeper to make it stronger.

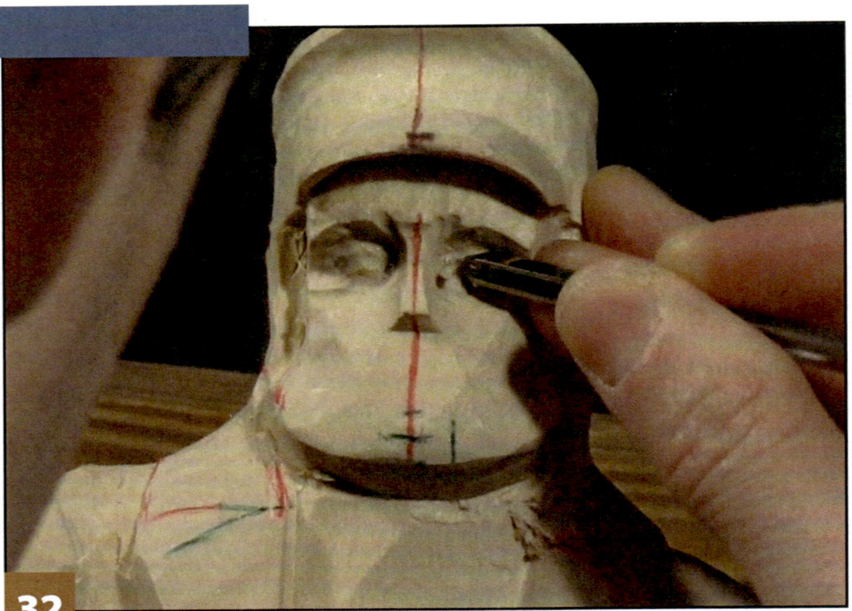

32 **Carve along the bottom of the eye area made in Step 7.** Use the ⅛" (3mm) #11 gouge. Start at the brow line and then carve downward, following the curve of the stop cut. Carve deep enough to remove all of the stop cut. The top edge of this cut defines the bottom eyelid. Then, carve a gouge mark across the top of the eye, from the outer canthus (corner of the eye) to the inner canthus. The bottom edge of this cut will form the upper eyelid, so make sure it is placed and shaped appropriately. Make sure that it's deep enough at the side of the nose so that you cannot see the inner canthus from the side when viewing the face in profile. To achieve the proper shape for the eye, you may need to tweak the cut under the eye and bring the end of it up to meet with the end of the cut you just made. Round the eye mound if necessary; you don't want to have a vertical ridge or corner in the center of the eye.

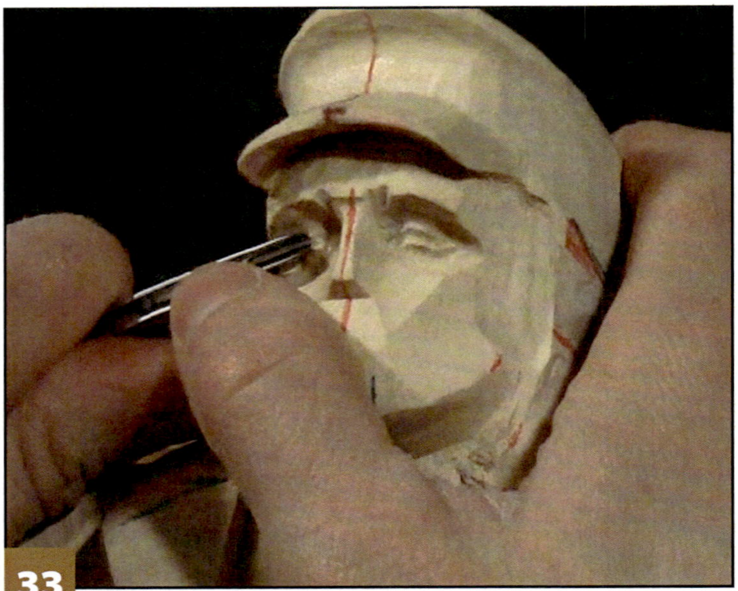

33 **Draw the shapes of the lids onto the eye mound.** For this size figure, the eyes should be ¼" (6mm) wide. Carve out between the lines for the upper and lower eyelids with the ⅛" (3mm) #11 gouge. Start at the outer edge of the eye and carve in toward the nose, following the curvature of the eye mound. At first it'll be a very light cut where the eyelid lines are close together. Then, you'll carve deeper as the eyelid lines become farther apart so that each side of the gouge's blade is touching one of the lines. As you get closer to the nose, the eyelid lines come together at the inner canthus so you'll have to lighten up the pressure and not carve as deeply as you finish the cut. At this point you should see two little ridges that create the vague form of an eye.

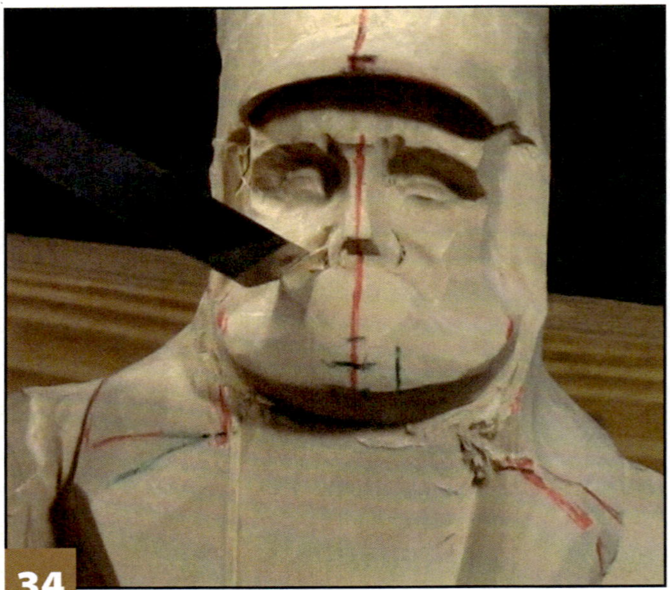

34 **Mark the 5⁄16" (8mm) width of the nostrils.** Make a stop cut along the outside with the ⅛" (3mm) #5 gouge. Rough in the smile lines with the ¼" (6mm) #11 gouge. Use the 5⁄16" (8mm) skew chisel or a knife to deepen the stop cuts made with the #5 gouge. Use the skew chisel to stop-cut into the smile line along where the top of the mustache will be. Carve from the smile line down to meet this stop cut and remove a three-sided chip out from beside each nostril. Use the 5⁄16" (8mm) #5 gouge to angle the bottom of each nostril up away from the center of the bottom of the nose.

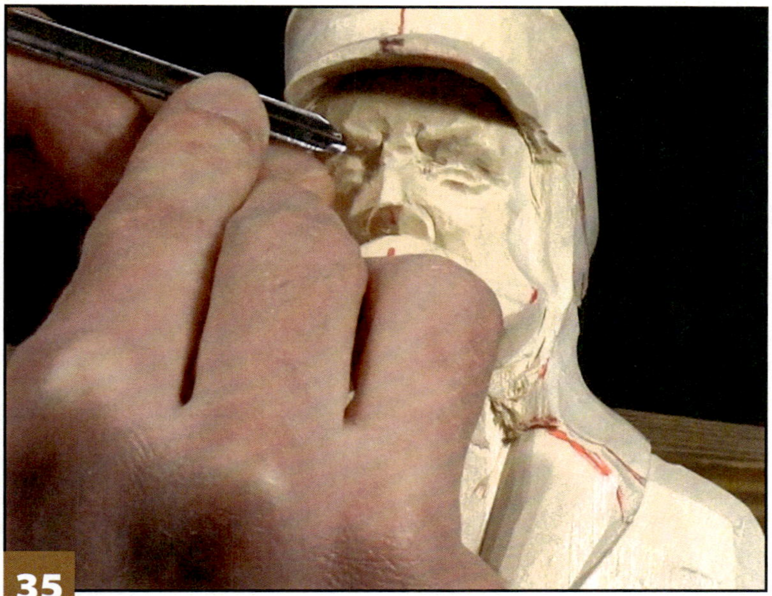

35 **Deepen the bridge of the nose and tweak the profile of the nose as desired.** Use the ⅛" (3mm) #11 gouge. Separate the temples from the cheekbones with a ½" (or 12mm) #5 gouge; this should narrow the width of the brow down to 1" (25mm). Use the 5⁄16" (8mm) #5 gouge to round the eyebrows. Set up a crease between the end of each eyebrow and the bridge of the nose by making a V-shaped cut with the same gouge. Give the eyebrow more expression and structure by carving across the ridge of the brow with the ⅛" (3mm) #11 gouge. Blend the edges of these cuts with the skew chisel. Create a slight depression above the eyebrows to separate the brows from the forehead. Round the corners of the forehead with the 5⁄16" (8mm) #5 gouge turned upside down.

36 **Divide the distance from the chin to the bottom of the nose into thirds.** The first mark below the nose is the part in the lips and is where the bottom of the center of the mustache should be. Draw the shape of the mustache. Stop-cut the bottom edge and the tips of the mustache, then tuck the lips and chin area under the mustache. Draw the bottom edge of the bottom lip halfway between the chin and nose. Use the ⅛" (3mm) #11 gouge to carve around the bottom edge of the lower lip. Tuck the corners of the lower lip in deep as it goes under the mustache. Just barely round the lower lip underneath the mustache.

37 **Round the top edge of the mustache into the smile line with the skew chisel or knife.** Blend the beard into the bottom of the gouge cut below the lower lip. Further accentuate the hollow of the cheeks by carving with the ¾" (19mm) #9 gouge from the corners of the mouth toward the ear. Carve an arc (think about a rainbow) underneath the lower lip with the ⅛" (3mm) #11 gouge. Deepen at the corners of the mouth, and then blend these cuts to finalize the shape of the lower lip.

38 **Draw a rectangle for the ears on both sides of the head.** Make the top of the rectangle level with the brow line and the bottom level with the bottom of the nose. The distance from the bottom of the chin to the center of the eyes (half the height of the head), is the same as from the tip of the nose to the front of the ear, which is how the front of the ear is located. Draw the shape of the ear inside of the rectangle. Use a V-tool to stop-cut the front edge of the ear, then use the 5⁄16" (8mm) #5 gouge to carve an angled plane into the sideburn to the depth of the side of the face. Stop-cut the sideburns at the bottom edge of the hat. Tuck the sideburns under the hat and blend them into the beard and the side of the face. Make sure that the sideburns do not totally block the view of the ears from the front. Stop-cut and clean out the bottom edge of the beard and the back of the ears.

REFINING THE FORMS

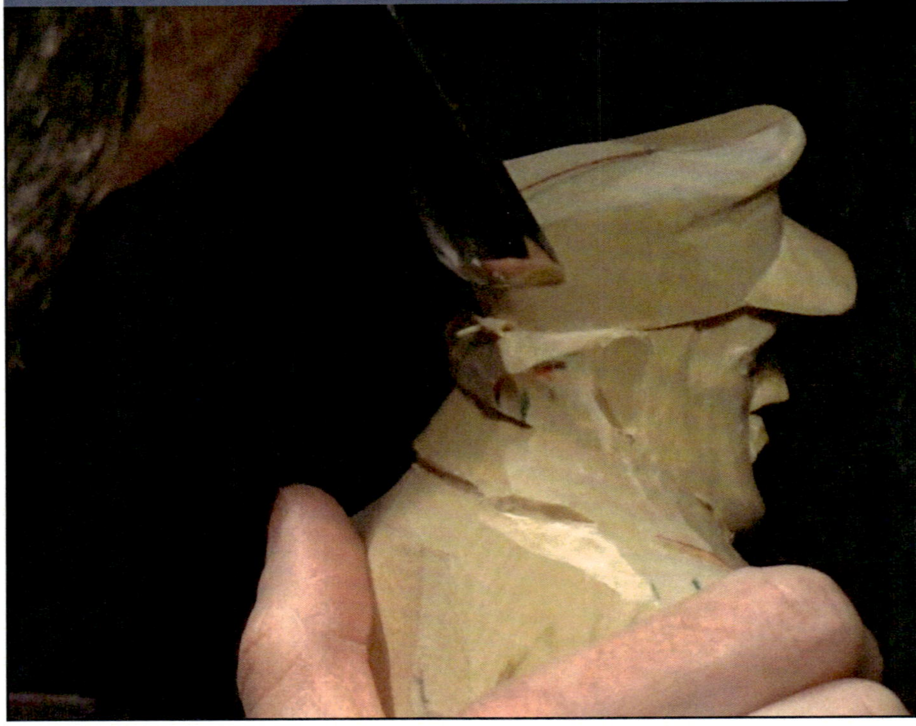

39 **Make a stop cut along the bottom edge of the hair.** Then, push the collar under the hair at the back of the neck. Stop-cut the bottom edge of the hat. Measure and mark from the tip of the nose one head height, 1¾ (4.4cm) on this carving, toward the back of the head and add ⅛" (3mm) for the hair. Then, shave off everything that sticks out beyond the mark to separate the head from the neck. Make this a vertical plane perpendicular to the centerline of the head. Draw the shape of the top of the hat. Stop-cut and narrow the bottom edge of the hat so that the ears stick out a little bit past the edge of the hat. Carve the shape of the back and sides of the hat with the 1" (25mm) #5 gouge from the top edge of the hat to its bottom edge. Do not knock off the ears or hair. Finish carving the depression around the crown of the hat. Draw the edge of the top of the hat, as seen from the side, and carve down to this with the ½" (13mm) #11 gouge. Further accentuate it with a cut from the ¼" (6mm) #11 gouge. Carve a slight depression on the back of the hat from one ear around to the other. The top edge of this cut is in the middle heightwise. Blend everything together with the skew chisel to complete the shaping of the hat.

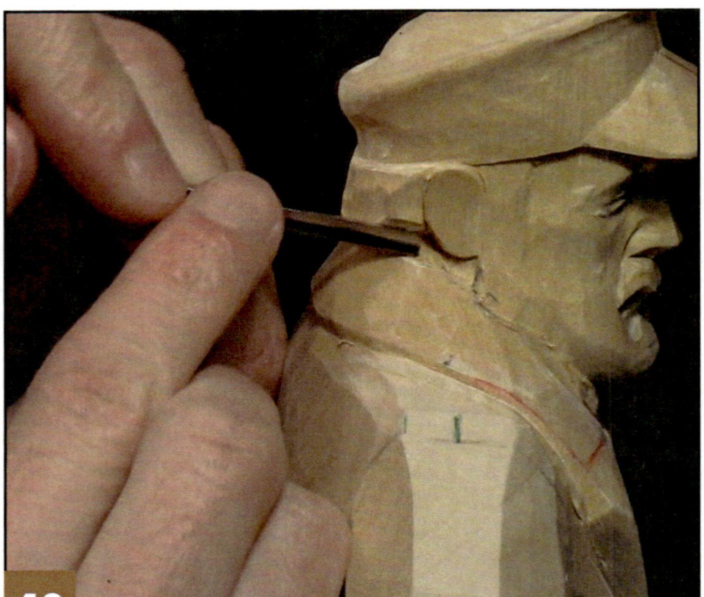

40 **Separate the edges of the collar from the beard.** Use the ¼" (6mm) V-tool. Keep in mind that the right side of the beard touches the collar just in front of the right ear. Carve down to the right side of the neck by making stop cuts along the hairline, around the right ear, across the top edge of the collar, and the beard at the corner of the jaw. Then, recess this area with the ⅛" (3mm) #5 gouge so that the thickness of the collar is 1⁄16" (2mm).

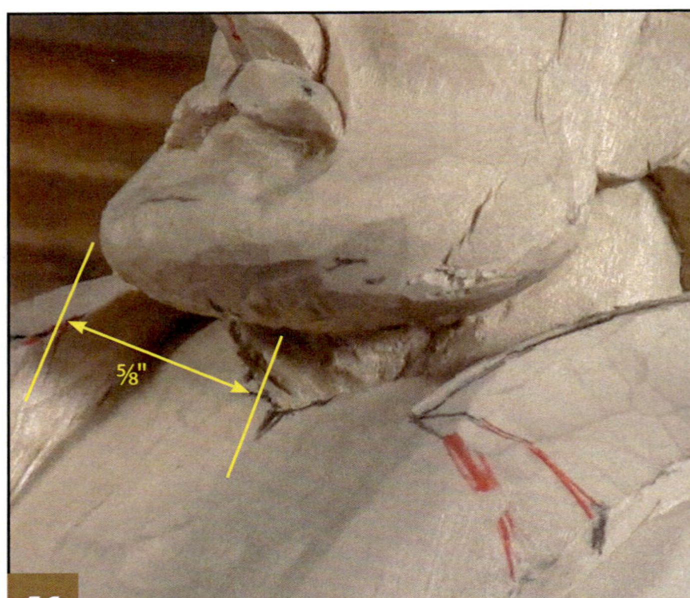

41 **Make a stop cut under the beard.** Angle the chest up to this stop cut. The base of the neck needs to be pushed back ⅝" (1.6cm) from the front of the beard. Undercut the bottom of the beard enough to carve the shirt collar. Push the shirt up over the shoulders and underneath the coat collar on both sides. Carve the recess on the left side of the neck to match the right side. Stop-cut the shirt collar and taper the throat behind the shirt. Use the ⅛" (3mm) #5 gouge and a 1⁄32" (1mm) #11 gouge for most of the carving, but a pair of 1⁄16" (2mm) spoon-bent skew chisels and sharpened dental picks work well in the tight areas. If all else fails, use a rotary tool with a small bit. To increase the realism of the carving, create depressions to bring out the sternomastoid muscle on the left side and the bottom of the Adam's apple. Cut out the notches that separate the collar from the lapels.

42 **Mark the widths for the fingers on the back of the left hand.** Curl each finger to the desired position by creating a plane for each joint of each finger with the 5⁄16" (8mm) #5 gouge. Let the index finger hang straight down and curl each finger successively more. Remember that as you move toward the tip, each finger joint is two-thirds the length of the one before. Once the fingers are positioned, trim them to length. Trim the outside edge of the pinky finger so that it's not quite as thick as the others.

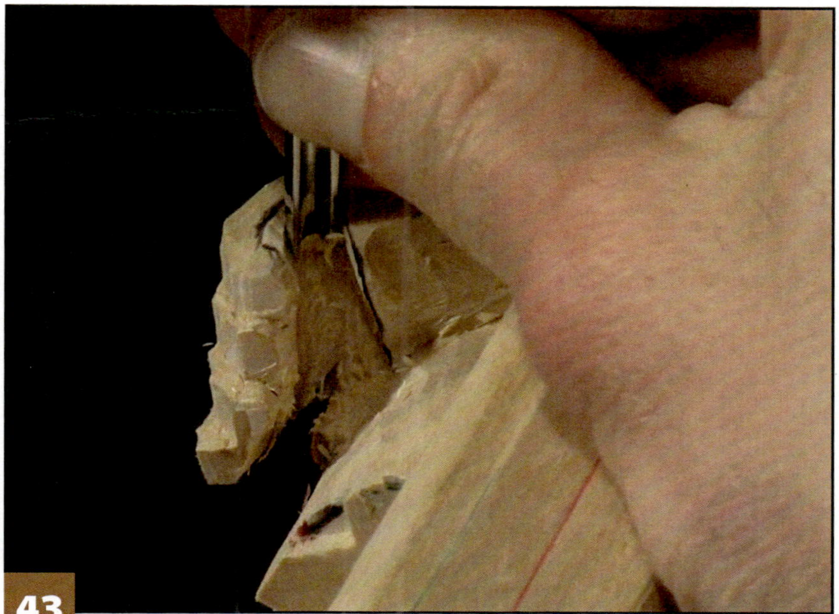

43 **Stop-cut between the side of the coat and the area of the base of the left thumb.** Use the ½" (13mm) #2 gouge. Then, carving from below, create the angle of the base of the thumb as it hangs down. Separate the top of the thumb from the coat with a 1⁄16" (2mm) V-tool. Create the space between the thumb and the fingers with the 1⁄32" (1mm) #11 gouge. Trim the thumb to length; the tip hangs down to a point that is halfway between the last two joints of the index finger. On the outside edge of the hand, draw the thickness of the pinky finger and the edge of the hand. Remove the waste on the inside of the fingers. Use the 1⁄32" (1mm) #11 gouge to get between the fingers and the cuff. Once the area has been opened up some, clean and shape this area with the ⅛" (3mm) #11 gouge and the ⅛" (3mm) #5 gouge.

44 **Carve the planes of the fingers of the right hand.** Repeat Steps 41 and 42. Do not accentuate the knuckles on the right hand with the 5⁄16" (8mm) #5 gouge yet.

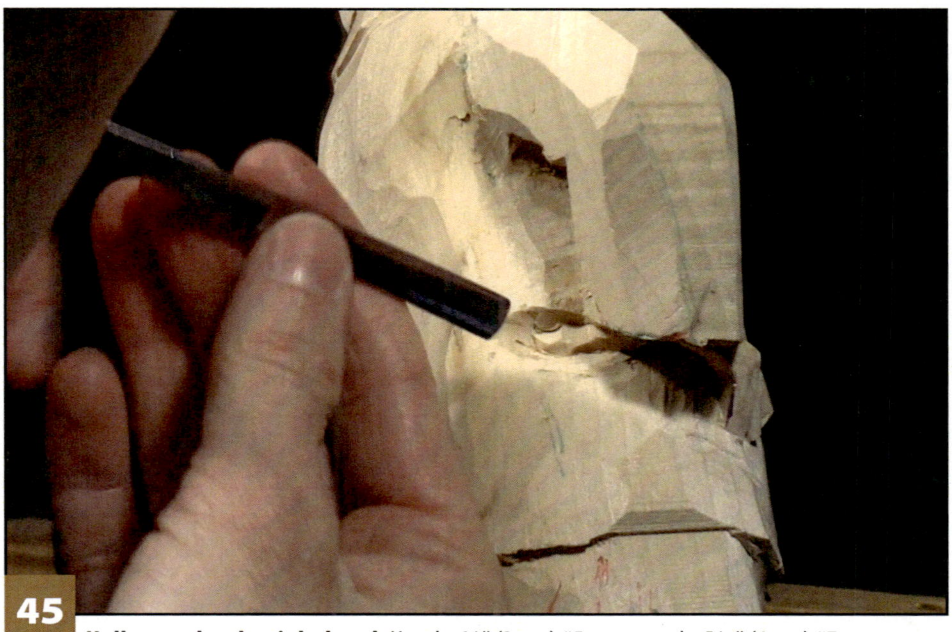

45 **Hollow under the right hand.** Use the ⅛" (3mm) #5 gouge and a 5⁄32" (4mm) #7 gouge. I found that hollowing this area helped me with positioning and shaping the thumb. When you pose the hand in this position, there is a hollow in the palm that runs from the center of the palm at the wrist, to the base of the index finger. Establish the pinky side of the palm of the hand. From the pinky side, measure 1 5⁄16" (3.3cm) to the tip of the thumb. Use the 5⁄16" (8mm) #5 gouge to help stop-cut and shape the planes of the thumb. Remember that the angle of the thumb to the side of the fingers can't exceed 90° and that the first knuckle of the thumb is halfway between the wrist and the knuckles of the fingers. Don't be afraid to press the tip of the thumb into the coat so that it is about 90° to the fingers; you may need to press the fingers into the coat as well.

REFINING THE FORMS

46 **Draw a rectangle on the bottom of the right shoe.** Make the shoe 2⅜" (6cm) long. Make the widest point of the toe 1" (2.5cm) and make the heel 13⁄16" (2.1cm) wide. Cut the foot to those dimensions first. Then, draw and carve the curved edges of the shoe to make it footprint-shaped. Round the toe with a ½" (or 12mm) #5 gouge. Use the skew chisel to do the final rounding and blending.

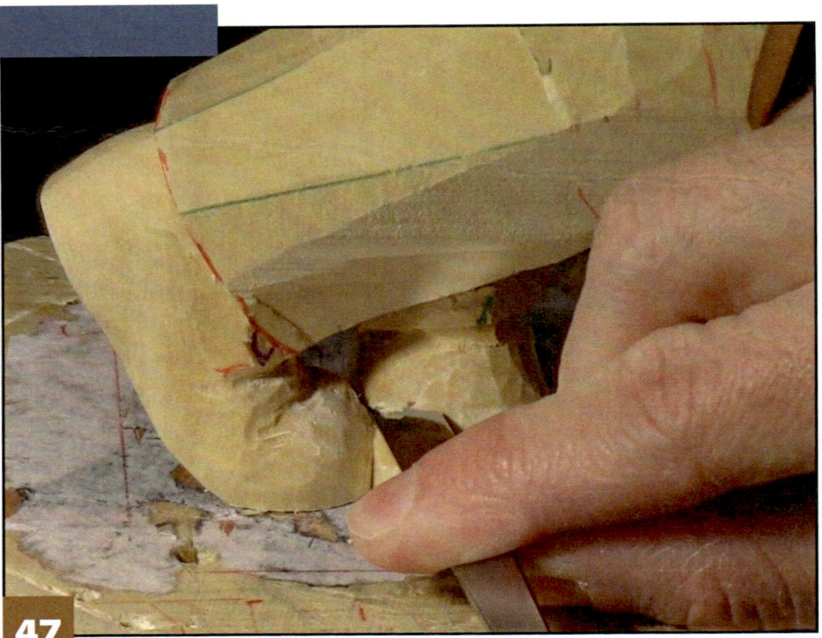

47 **Adjust the angle of the sole of the left shoe so that it is the same dimensions as the right shoe.** Stop-cut the end of the pants with a V-tool. Then, cut the shoe into the shape of the footprint. Wrap the shape of the top of the toe into the area between the feet that will need to be pierced. Then, drill through the area to pierce with a 3⁄16" (5mm)-diameter bit. Wrap the cuff of the right leg through this opening with the skew chisel and knife. This will allow the rest of the top of the right shoe to be shaped. Shape the rest of the left shoe by enlarging and working through the pierced area.

48 **Measure and carve both legs to their final widths.** Use the 1" (25mm) #2 gouge. Make sure that the right leg is centered over the shoe. Some planes will have to be adjusted as you add the final planes of the leg where the left leg presses into the shin of the right leg. Undercut the left shin to create a ridge of fabric that hangs down off the shin. Begin separating between the legs with the ¼" (6mm) V-tool. Because the finished opening isn't much larger than ⅛" (3mm), use a 1⁄16" (2mm)-diameter bit to drill through the wood between the legs. This time we can't drill straight through the block of wood; instead drill in at a 40° to 45° angle. Drill the first hole behind the left knee and check where it comes out on the back before drilling more holes. Drill a hole every ¼" (6mm) up to the crotch. Use the 1⁄32" (1mm) #11 gouge and the knife to carve away the wood between the legs.

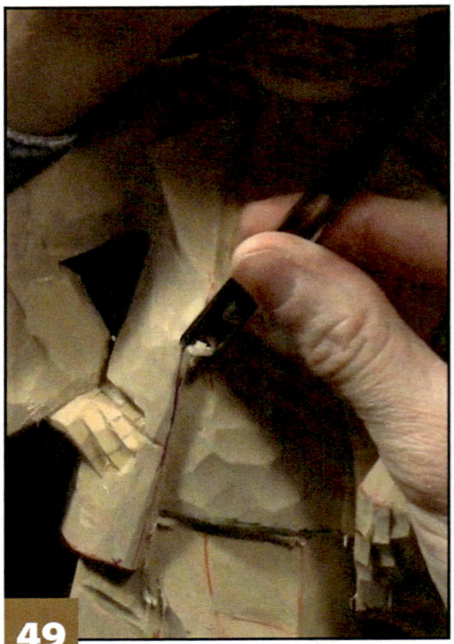

49 **Trim the bottom edge of the coat to length.** The highest point of the coat's bottom edge is at the right hip, and it slopes down to each corner from there. Make the left corner the lowest point. Add the slight curve to the right edge of the coat by the buttons, and recess the shirt if necessary.

Adding the Details

TIP

CARVE IN PAIRS

The best way to carve a matching pair of something (like the eyes) is to carve them together, making the same cut on each side before making the next cut.

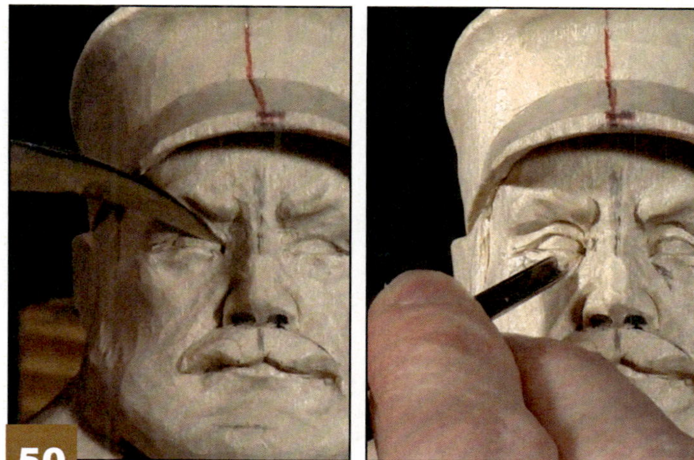

50 **Make a gouge cut that starts at the inner canthus and runs roughly parallel to the smile line until it blends out into the hollow of the cheek.** Use the 5/16" (8mm) #5 gouge. This separates the smile line from the cheekbones and removes the puffy, saggy look from the cheeks. As you blend this cut out, refine the smile lines so that almost all of the nostril can be seen in profile. Stop-cut the upper eyelid with the 5/16" (8mm) #5 gouge along the ridge that forms the upper lid. Use the knife to carve from the lower eyelid to the upper eyelid to clean out the stop cut. Next stop-cut and then clean out the lower lid. When doing the clean-out cut, make sure you place the knife tip right underneath the upper eyelid and carve from there to the stop cut at the lower lid so that when looking at the eye in profile, it has a slight down and inward angle to it. Use the tip of the knife to take a small three-sided chip out of both corners of the eye to give it more depth and roundness. Don't be surprised if you have to do a little blending to round the eyeball into the corners. Carve the crease above the eye with a 1/8" (3mm) V-tool. Use the same V-tool to add some wrinkles under the eye. Repeat for the other eye.

51 **Thin the bridge of the nose.** Use an appropriately sized #5 gouge to create a slight depression across the edge and top of the wings of the nostrils. The smile line wraps around into this area as it fades out above the nostril. Tweak the profile of the nose as desired. Carve the mustache and eyebrow hair by making V-cuts with the 5/16" (8mm) #5 gouge. Create the nostril openings with the 1/32" (1mm) #11 gouge. Round the front edge of the hat bill since the face has now been carved.

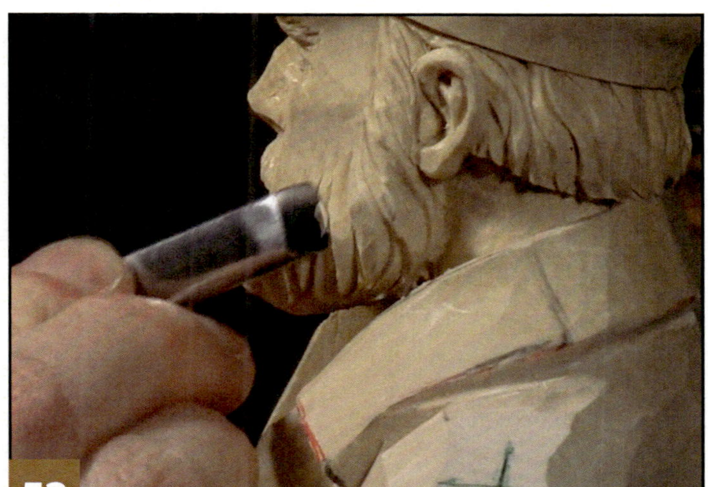

52 **Hollow the inside of each ear.** Then, on each ear, separate the outer curl (the helix) from the inner ridge (the anti-helix). Use the 1/16" (2mm) V-tool. Wrap the leg of the helix down into the ear. Just barely recess the antihelix into the ear, and then carve the upper groove inside the antihelix (the triangular fossa). Undercut each earlobe. Detail the beard and hair by making S-shaped V-cuts with the 5/16" (8mm) #5 gouge. Alternate the direction that you clean the cuts out from to create a varied texture. Use the 1/8" (3mm) #5 gouge to create tighter curves at the ends of the hair.

ADDING THE DETAILS

53 **Bend a small wire to the shape of the right edge of the coat.** Mark the bottom corner of the coat on the wire and mark where the lapel blends into the edge of the coat. Straighten the wire and measure and mark three equally spaced points between the two marks for the three coat buttons. Bend the wire back to match the edge of the coat and transfer the marks to the carving to note the location of the buttons. Use the wire to lay out the locations of the buttonholes on the left edge of the coat in the same manner. This puts the buttons and the buttonholes in the correct positions despite the contours of the coat. Make stop cuts around the buttons with a $\frac{3}{16}$" (5mm) #9 gouge and carve up to the stop cuts to create a recess around them. Use a V-tool to carve $\frac{1}{4}$" (6mm)-long V-cuts for the buttonholes.

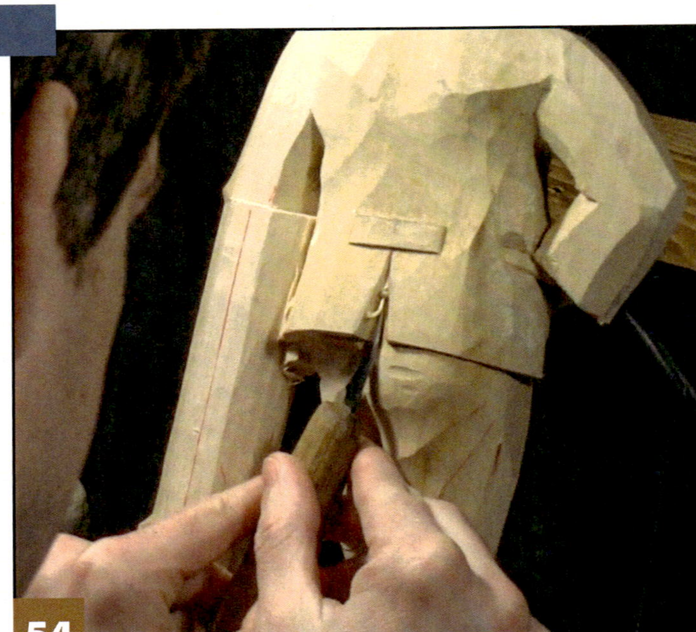

54 **Draw the belt on the back of the coat.** Make a stop cut around it with the $\frac{1}{16}$" (2mm) V-tool and then recess the coat around it. Stop-cut the split of the back of the coat and recess that area by $\frac{1}{16}$" (2mm). Draw the bottom edge of the shirt and make a stop cut along that line. Then, recess to the level of the pants, about $\frac{1}{16}$" (2mm). Carve the $\frac{1}{8}$" (3mm)-diameter buttons on the belt. Use the $\frac{3}{4}$" (19mm) #9 gouge, the $\frac{1}{2}$" (13mm) and $\frac{5}{16}$" (8mm) #5 gouges, and the skew chisel to give the collar and the lapels their final shape. Use a $\frac{1}{4}$" (6mm) #11 gouge and the $\frac{1}{8}$" (3mm) #11 gouge to give the right lapel the flag-wave shape.

55 **Mark the wrinkles and folds in the carving.** I use a red gel pen for the high points of the wrinkles and purple for the deep areas. This will make it easier to keep track of what needs to be done on the carving as you go along. I also draw the wrinkles onto the carving in sections (e.g., one arm or the thigh of one leg), so that things remain manageable. I use a variety of tools to carve the wrinkles, but I use the #11 gouges a lot. In general gouge out the deep areas between the ridges of cloth with a gouge of the appropriate size and sweep, and then blend. Keep in mind that there are a surprisingly large number of straight lines and planes in the wrinkle patterns of the clothes. Do not carve so deep that you cut through the clothes and into the body.

56 **Add wrinkles to the shirt.** Different fabrics fold and wrinkle differently. This is most noticeable with the shirt because it is a softer, thinner material than the coat or pants. Make these wrinkles shallow and more rounded.

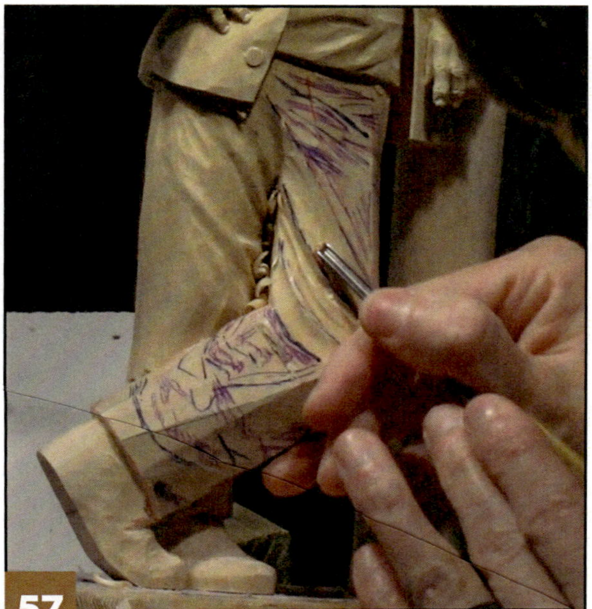

57 **Carve the wrinkles on the front of the pants.** Carve on each side of the wrinkle with a ¼" (6mm) or ⅛" (3mm) #11 gouge. Then, flatten the area between the gouge cuts.

58 **Make a ⅛" (3mm)-deep stop cut along the top edge of the rope on the post's back, the inside edge, and the plane between them.** Carve down ⅛" (3mm) with a V-tool. Then, use the V-tool to carve ⅛" (3mm)-deep marks about every 1" (2.5cm) or less all the way up each of these planes. The V-tool marks help keep things straight as you carve ⅛" (3mm) off of these sides of the post with the 1" (25mm) #2 gouge to separate the rope from the post. Carve off the corners of the post, and continue removing the sharp corners until the post is round. Where you can fit it in, use the ½" (or 12mm) #5 gouge upside-down to help round the post.

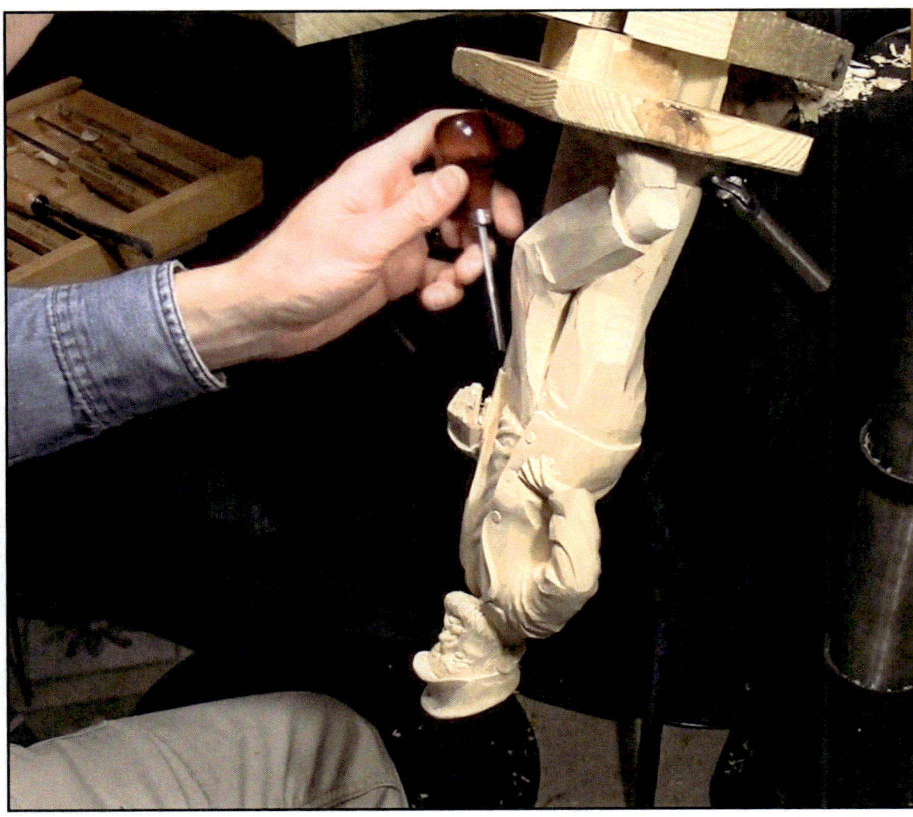

59 **Make sure that the section of coat below the left forearm angles to meet the side of the coat visible above the left forearm.** I pierced through the wood from below the left forearm into the area between the body and the upper arm while undercutting the bottom of the left forearm. Round the side of the top of the post in this area; use the spoon-bent skew chisels. There is a huge amount of wood that has to be removed as you undercut the bottom edge of the left side of the coat. Use the ⁵⁄₁₆" (8mm) #5 gouge to remove the bulk of the wood. Then, switch to other tools, like the ½" (or 12mm) #5 gouge and carving knives, to smooth the under/inside of the coat. Use the knife and the ¹⁄₃₂" (1mm) #11 gouge to undercut the left side of the coat and separate it from the left side of the body. I turned the carving upside down. To further hollow the inside of the coat, use a ⅛" (3mm) #5 palm tool. The shorter length of this tool allowed me to get it between the bottom edge of the coat and the board I mounted the carving on. Use the spoon-bent skew chisels to wrap the shirt around the left side of the body into the undercut of the edge of the coat. Do not try to undercut deeper than you have tools to clean the cut out with. The right side of the coat only requires a small undercut, for which I use the knife.

ADDING THE DETAILS

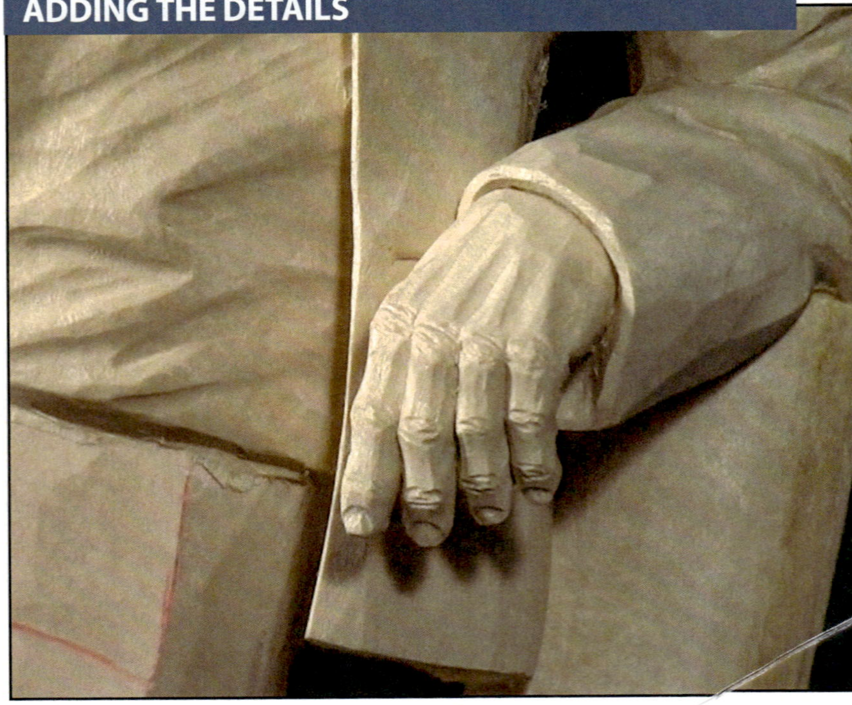

60 **Remove the corners from each plane of each finger with the 5/16" (8mm) #5 gouge.** This is all the rounding that the fingers need. The shape of this gouge helps to accentuate the knuckles, so in areas that this gouge doesn't work very well (like on the end grain), create the shape of this gouge's cut with a different tool, such as a knife. Taper the tips of each finger with the same gouge turned upside down. The tendons on the back of the hand are defined by carving between them with the 1/8" (3mm) #5 gouge, because the tendons are not very prominent in the positions of this figure. Make a cut on the corner of the hand with the same gouge just behind the first pinky knuckle, and then make another cut in front of the wrist to accentuate the fleshy area on the pinky side of the edge of the hand. Make similar cuts on the index finger side of the back of the hand to bring out the egg-shaped muscle between the index finger and the thumb. Cut between each of the first knuckles with the 1/16" (2mm) V-tool to give them more definition. Blend the cuts of the back of the hand, including the knuckles. Use the V-tool to cut wrinkle lines into all the knuckles and to wrap the finger pad creases around the side of the pinky and index fingers.

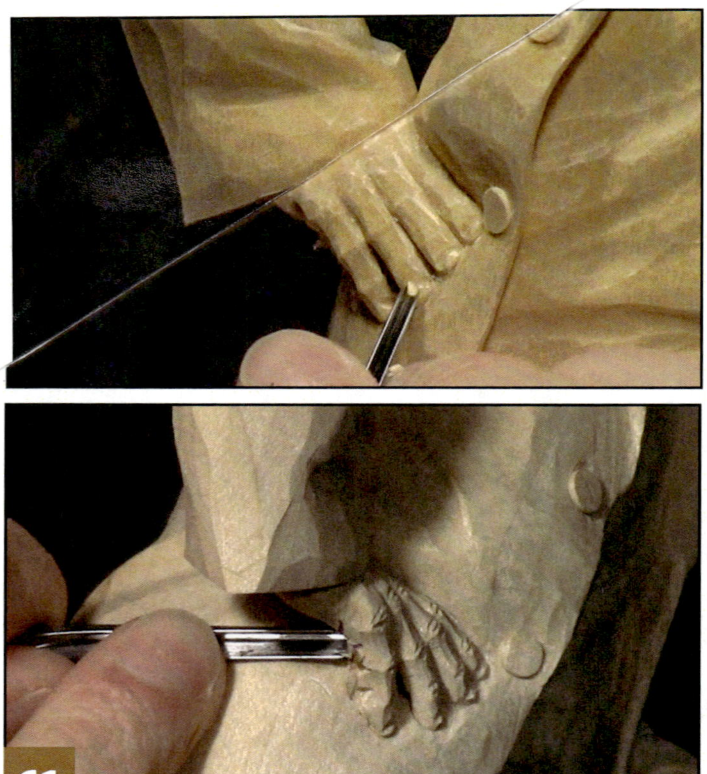

61 **Create the fingernails.** Carve an arch on each fingertip with the 1/32" (1mm) #11 gouge laid on its side. Use the 1/8" (3mm) #5 gouge upside down and carving knives to shape the inside (palm side) of the fingers as best you can. Make sure the fingertips are the right thickness. The back of the right thumb is carved similar to the back of the fingers, while the inside of the left thumb (which is all you see of it) is simply rounded and has a crease between the finger pads. Hollow the end of the sleeve.

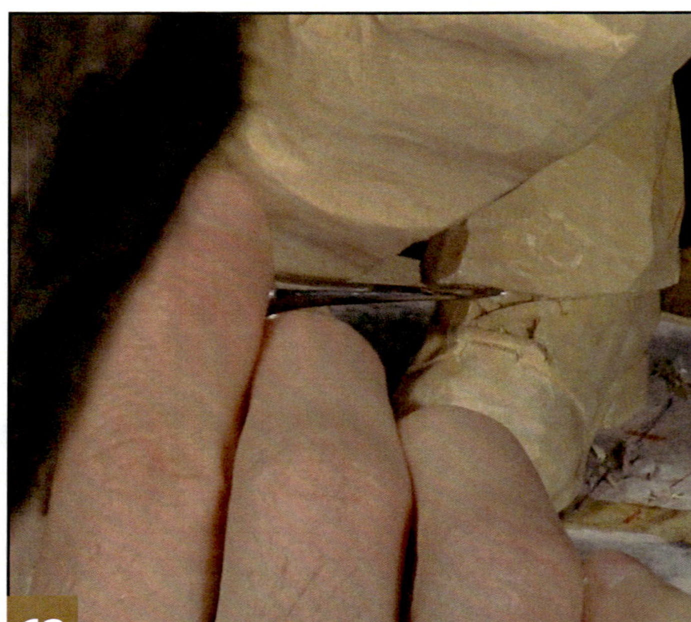

62 **Carve the notch in the sole of the shoes in front of the heels.** Stop-cut the edge of the sole and wrap the leather of the shoe upper into the bottom of this stop cut. Draw the laces and the edges of the quarter (the piece of leather that laps over the leather of the toe on the side of the shoe). Recess the top of the shoe around the laces leaving a raised rectangle of wood that the laces will be carved into. Redraw, and stop-cut the edges of the quarter, and then recess the toe to lap under the quarter and the laces. Stop-cut around the laces.

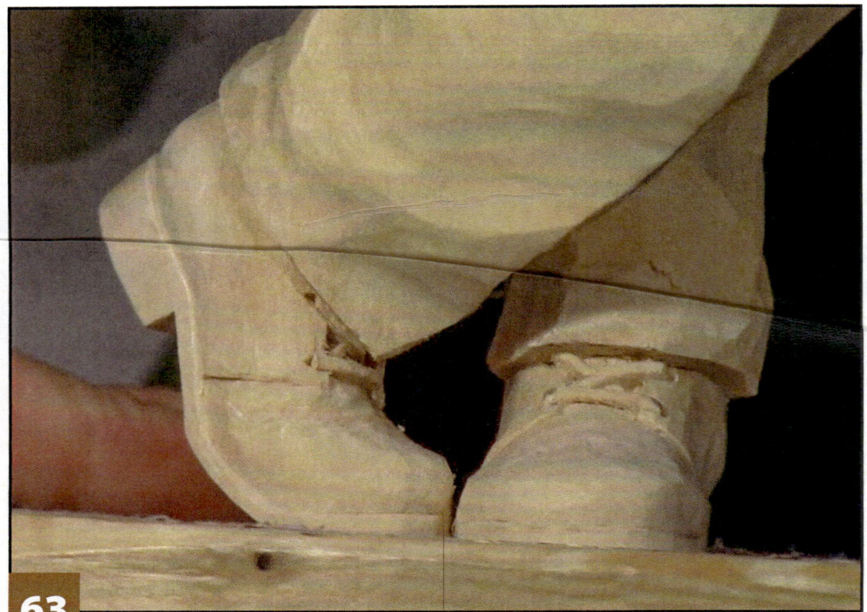

63 **Recess the triangles of wood between the laces down to the level of the shoe leather.** Some of this can be done with the tip of the knife, but some areas will take a very small tool such as a dental pick that has been sharpened into a chisel. Angle each of the laces so that one end laps under the leather of the shoe. One of the laces will have to be lapped under the other. Next stop-cut and chip out around the laces to get down to the level of the tongue of the shoe. Finish it off by making a tiny hole at the end of each lace for the eyelets of the shoes.

64 **Draw the tread pattern on the bottom of the left shoe.** Notch out the lugs around the edge of the sole and recess the pattern in the center. Remember to notch the edge of the right shoe sole and the toe of the left shoe where it's touching the ground as you need to see the tread pattern from the side.

Diagram 1

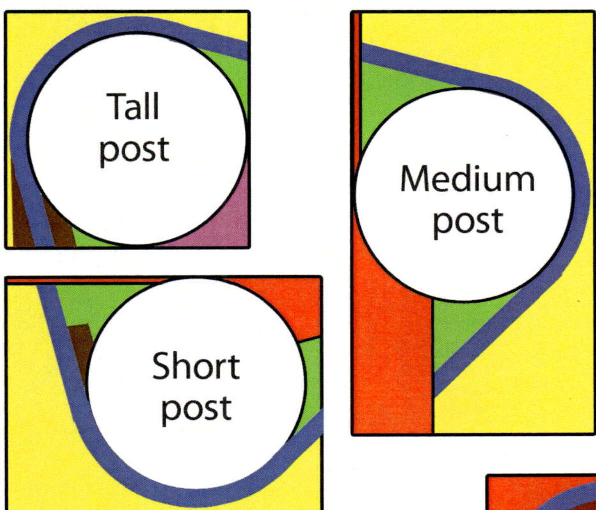

65 **These drawings show the blocks that the posts are carved from as seen from above.** The block marked as the Tall Post is the post that is part of the carving already, and in both diagrams the wood for the rope is the blue areas. Stop-cut along the top of the rope, which is 1⅞" (4.8cm) from the ground, and along the bottom of the rope, which is 1⅛" (2.9cm) from the ground. Carve the point on the end of the medium post with a knife. The area colored in red in diagram 1 on the medium and short post must be carved away. The pink area on the tall post should already have been removed. Diagram 2 shows how the blocks for the posts now fit together. Take great care to make these pieces fit together without gaps. Carve away the areas shown in green on Diagram 1. Glue the posts together with cyanoacrylate (CA) glue. Carve away the yellow areas to wrap the rope around the posts. The brown areas in Diagram 1 show where wood needs to be saved for the ends of the rope. Drill at an angle from the bottom of each post into one of the other posts, and then glue a toothpick in this hole. Repeat so that each post is pegged to both of its neighbors. This strengthens the joints of the posts that have been added.

Diagram 2

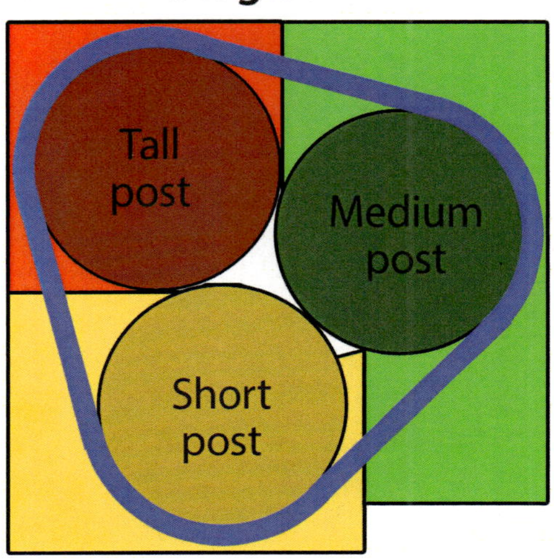

ADDING THE DETAILS

66 **Draw the rope as it wraps around the posts and lay out how the ends of the rope tuck through and behind.** Where the rope tucks through on the bottom, stop-cut around the rope where it crosses over the run of rope above it before tucking through. Relieve away around this section, leaving it raised while all the rest of the rope runs straight from the side of one post to the next. Carve a split between the ropes on both sides of where the rope tucks through.

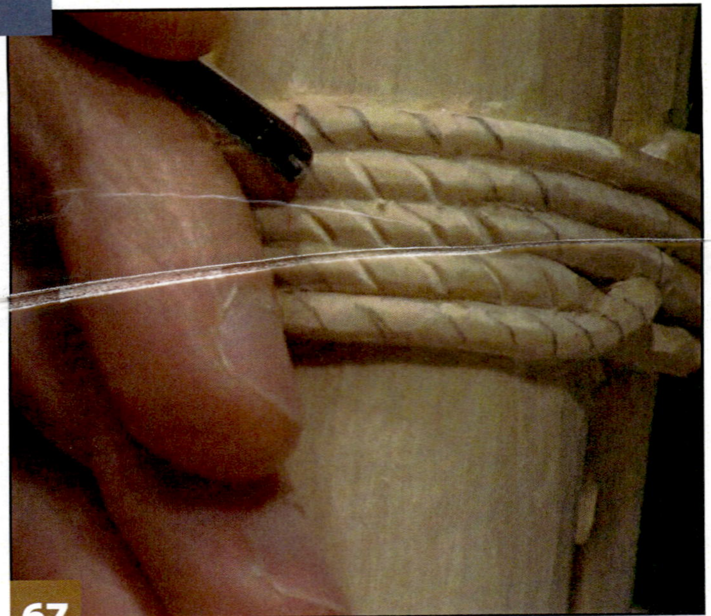

67 **Use a V-tool to carve a groove on the line between each rope.** Work to make the rope the same thickness throughout. Round the rope with the 1⁄8" (3mm) #5 gouge turned upside down. Use the 1⁄16" (2mm) V-tool to make diagonal cuts to create the rope texture. Give the entire carving a light sanding with 320 grit. This is just to knock the edges off of the tool marks. Some of the crevices will need more serious attention. Diamond rifflers, dental picks, sanding sticks and power carving bits will allow these areas to be cleaned out.

Painting the Captain

Unless otherwise noted, I paint working from transparent to opaque colors and from light to dark colors

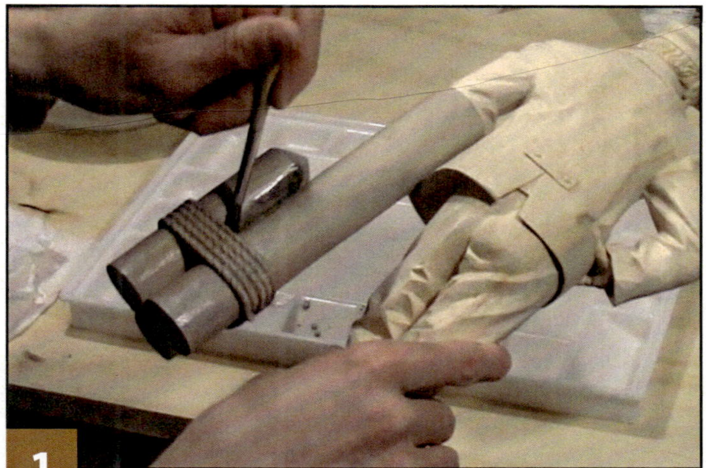

1 **Paint the posts and rope with a few coats of watery gray.** Add the shadows around and behind the rope and between the posts with watery black.

TIP

WET-INTO-WET BLENDING

To subtly blend shadows into the main color, such as on the pants, use the wet-into-wet painting technique. Apply the base color (for the pants, unbleached titanium) to the carving and then apply the shadow color (burnt umber) to the deep wrinkles while the base color is still wet. Brush back and forth across the deep shadows to blend the shadow color with the rest of the colors. Pick up the base color on the brush and add as needed to tone down the shadow color and create a smooth transition of color.

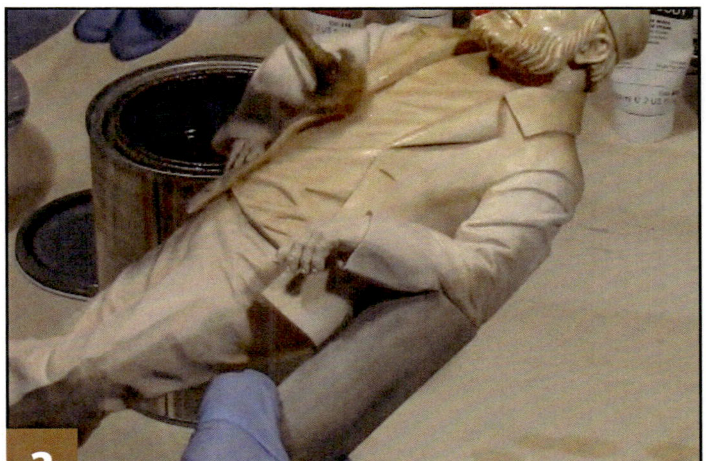

2 **Seal the carving.** Apply a single good coat of Bullseye Sealcoat. Allow it to dry.

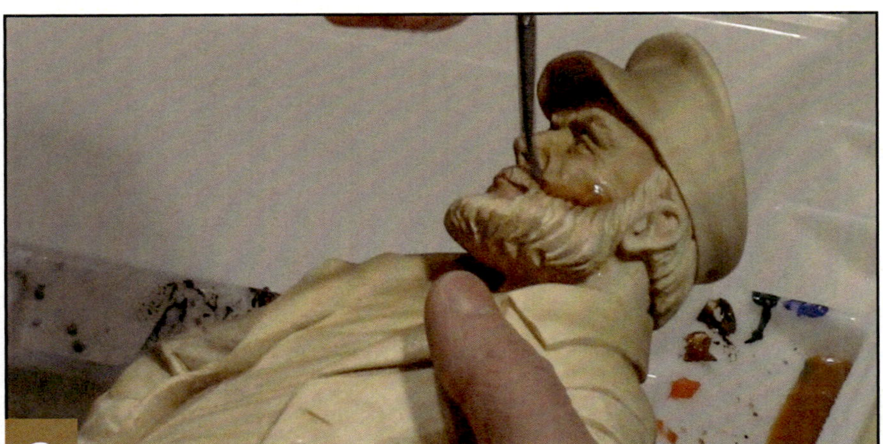

3 **Leave the exposed flesh the natural color of the basswood.** Thin burnt sienna heavily with water and add a tiny bit of vermilion. Apply this wash to the crevices of the face and hands. Multiple coats will be required to build up the necessary color. Keep this paint out of the highlight areas of the face: the cheekbones, tip of the nose, center of forehead, and the chin. Remember to add shadows to the ears and neck.

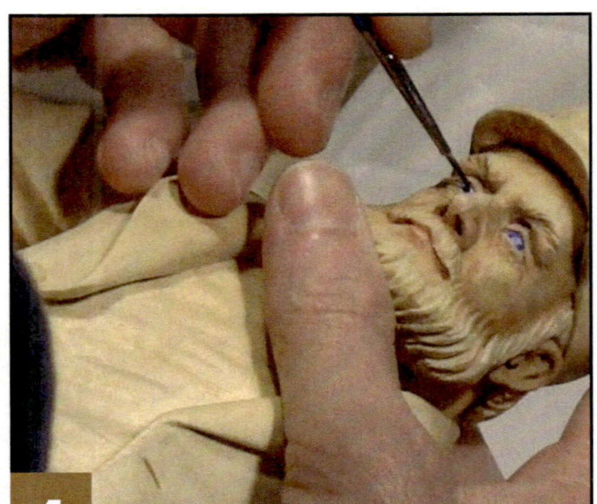

4 **Paint the eyes white.** Then, paint the irises ultramarine blue. Paint the reflected light in the irises cerulean blue. Paint the pupils black, and add specks of white for the highlights.

PAINTING THE CAPTAIN

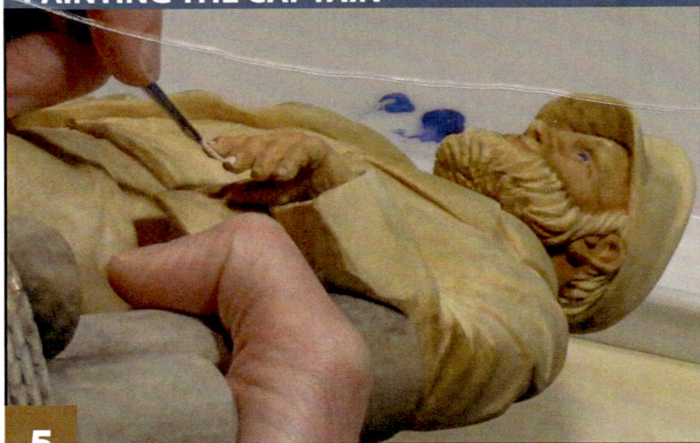

5 **Mix titanium white, vermilion, and burnt umber.** This creates a very pale peach color for the fingernails.

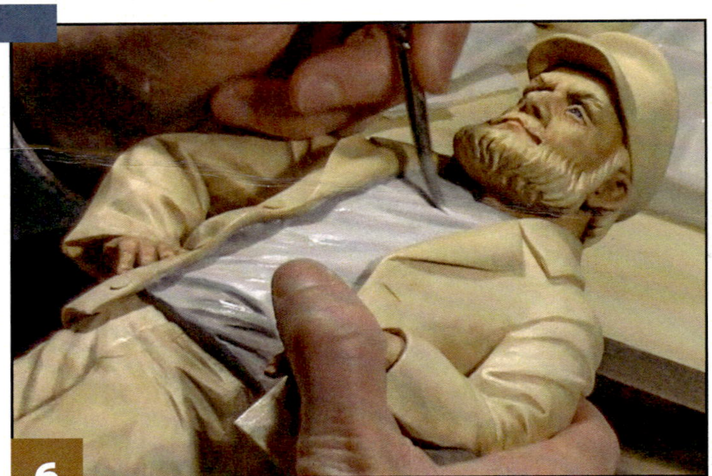

6 **Paint the shirt with titanium white.** Then, add shadows with gray.

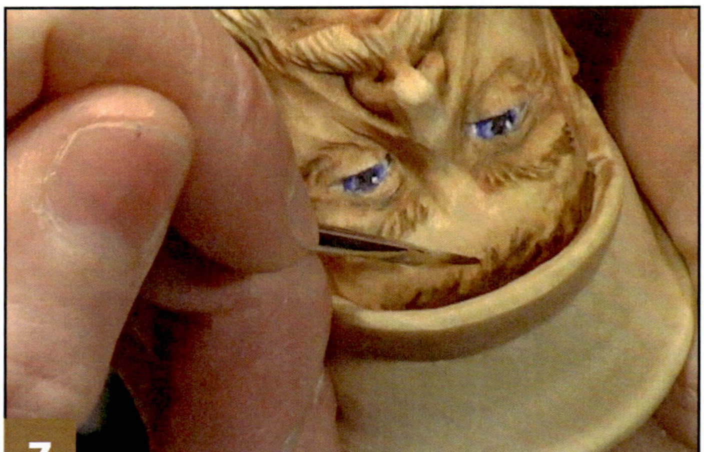

7 **Create the shadows under the hat bill.** Use burnt umber and black. Use the same color to add a few stray hairs.

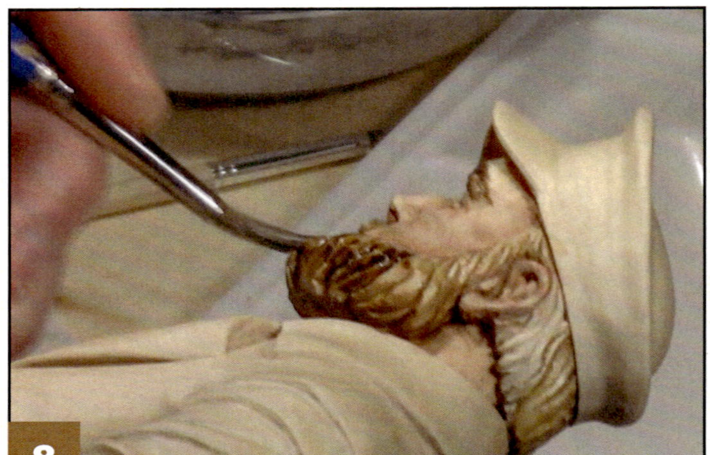

8 **Apply a couple of coats of burnt umber wash to the beard, mustache, and hair.** Dry-brush the eyebrows with burnt umber.

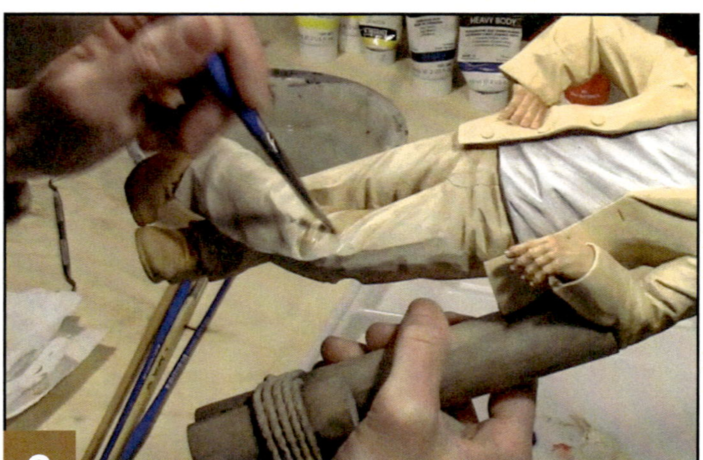

9 **Paint the pants with a coat of unbleached titanium.** Then, shadow the creases with a mixture of burnt umber and unbleached titanium. Blend onto the legs using the wet-into-wet blending technique (see page 25).

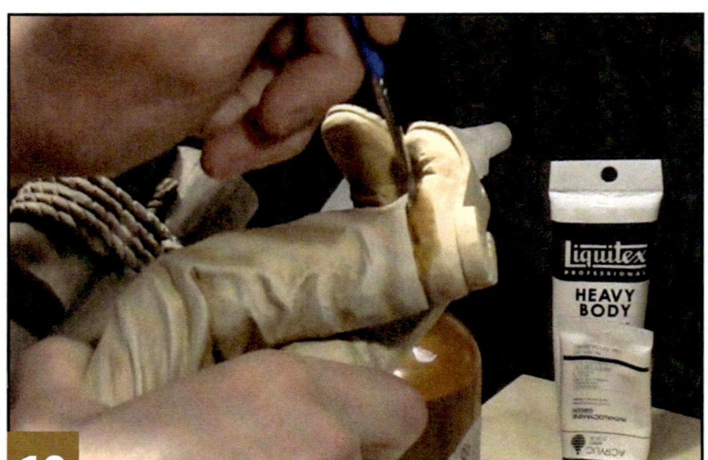

10 **Apply a coat of watered-down burnt umber to the leather of the shoes.** Apply two or three coats of burnt umber to the shoelaces.

11 **Paint the shoe soles with several coats of thinned black.** Make sure the color builds up to make a solid black color.

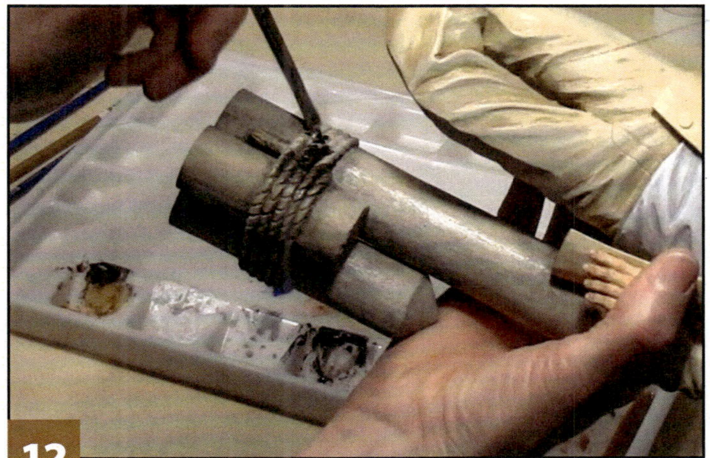

12 **Paint the ropes with heavily thinned gray.** It should be thin enough to flow into the texture of the ropes. Let the gray dry, and then dry-brush the ropes with unbleached titanium.

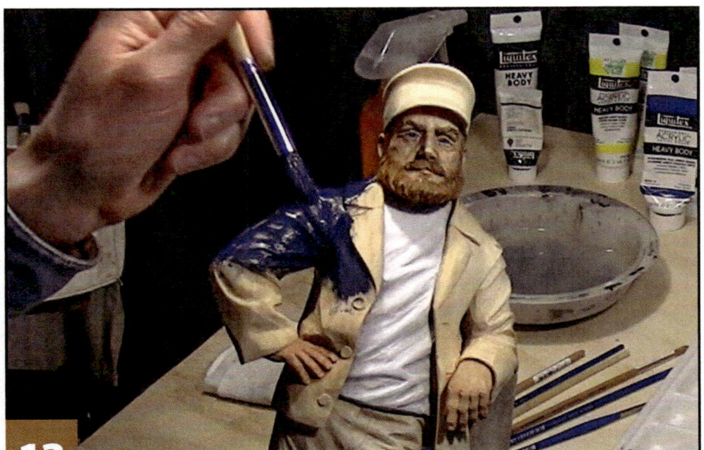

13 **Mix 3 parts ultramarine blue and 1 part black.** Apply it to the coat and hat. Add some white to this mix to dry-brush the highlights on the coat with a large paintbrush.

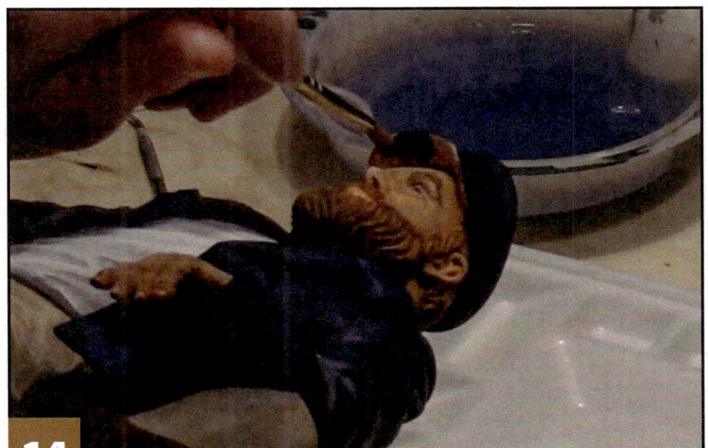

14 **Paint the bill of the hat black.**

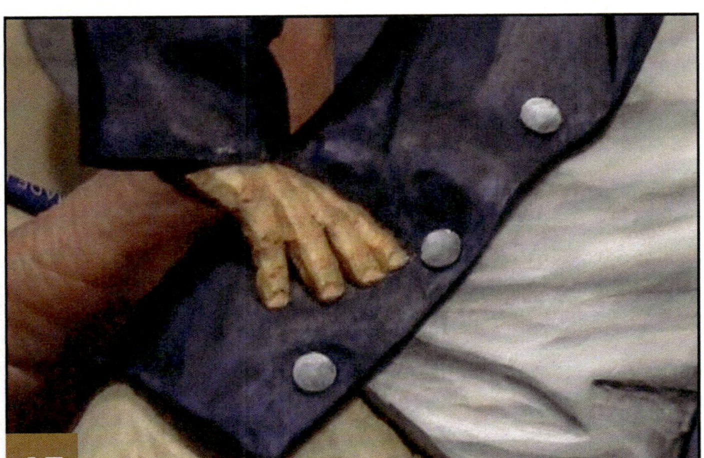

15 **Use the wet-into-wet painting (see page 25) technique to paint the coat buttons.** Blend black and white to create the highlights and shadows on the buttons. This will give them a steel look.

16 **Apply a clear finish.** Spray with a couple coats of a water-based acrylic finish to help protect the paint from wear.

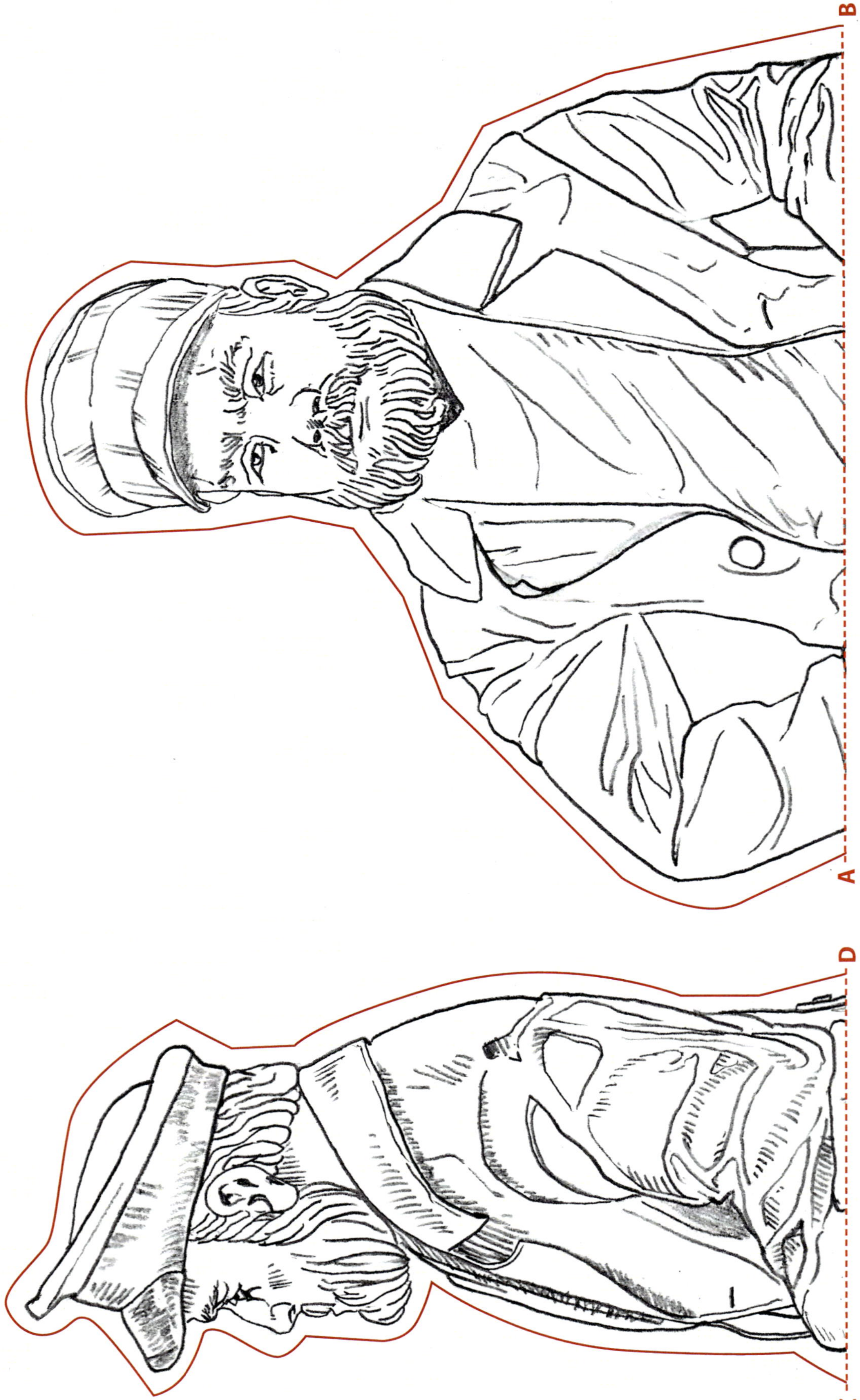
B
A
D
C

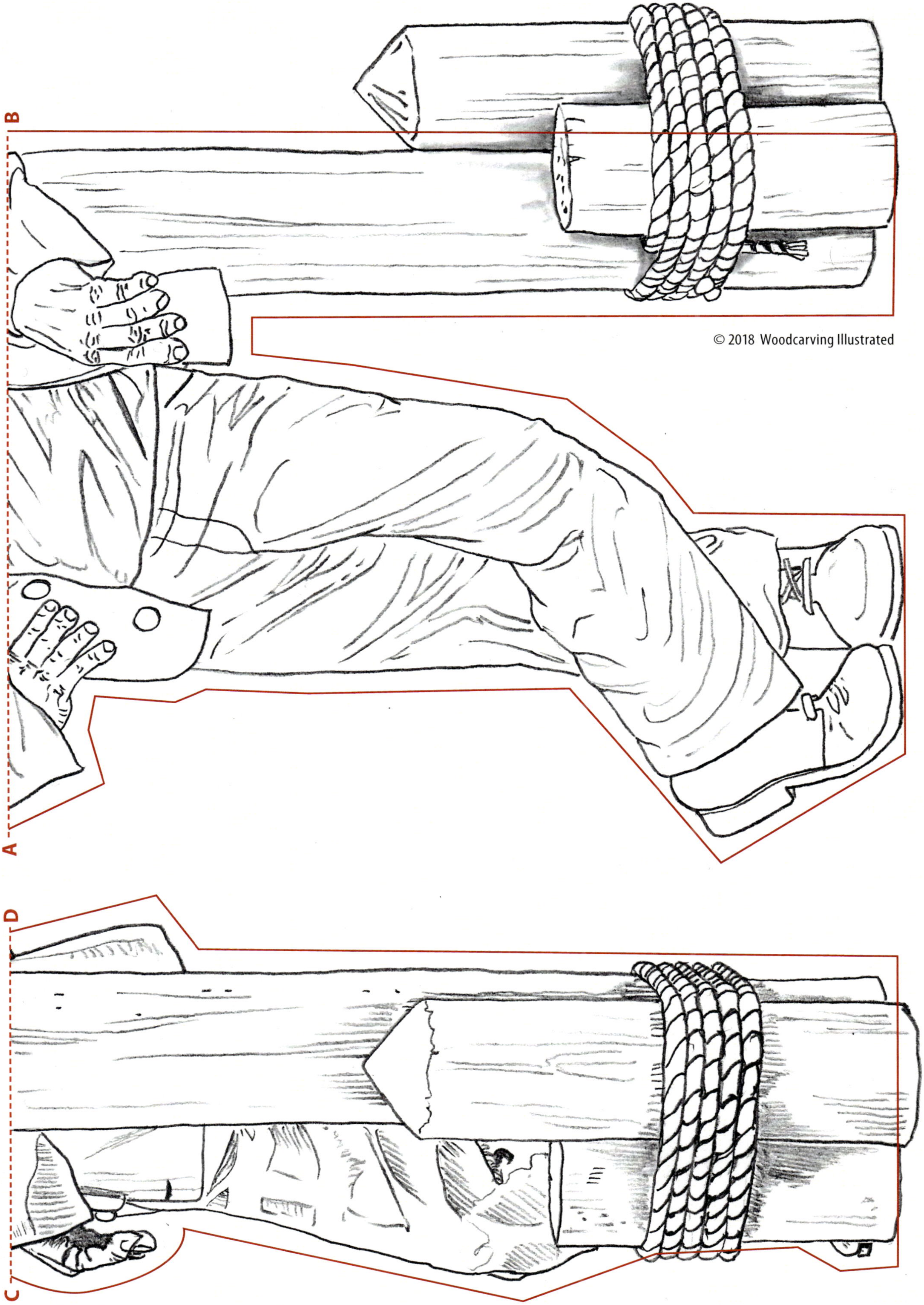
B
A
D
C

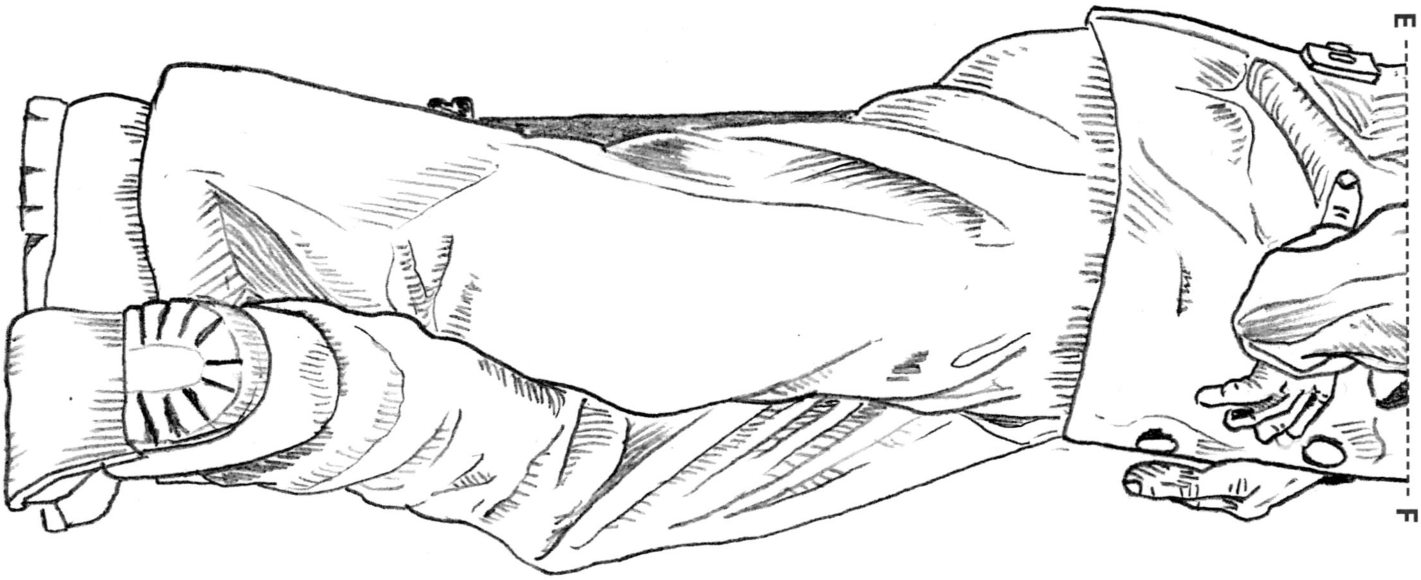
E
F

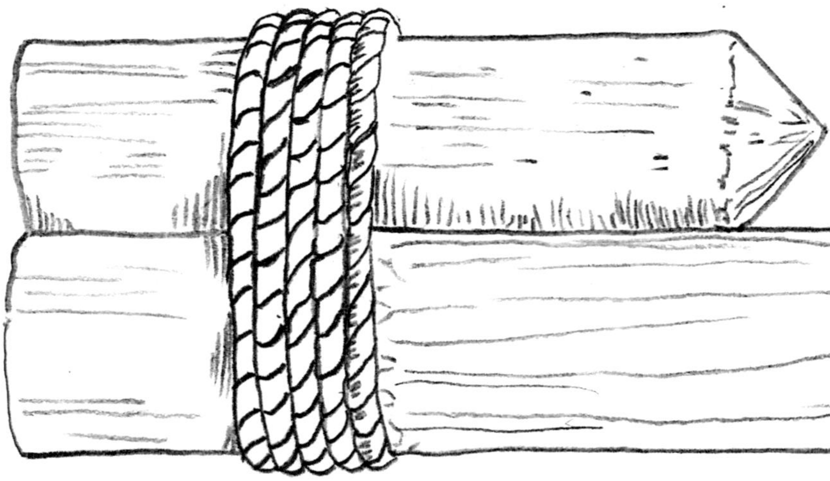

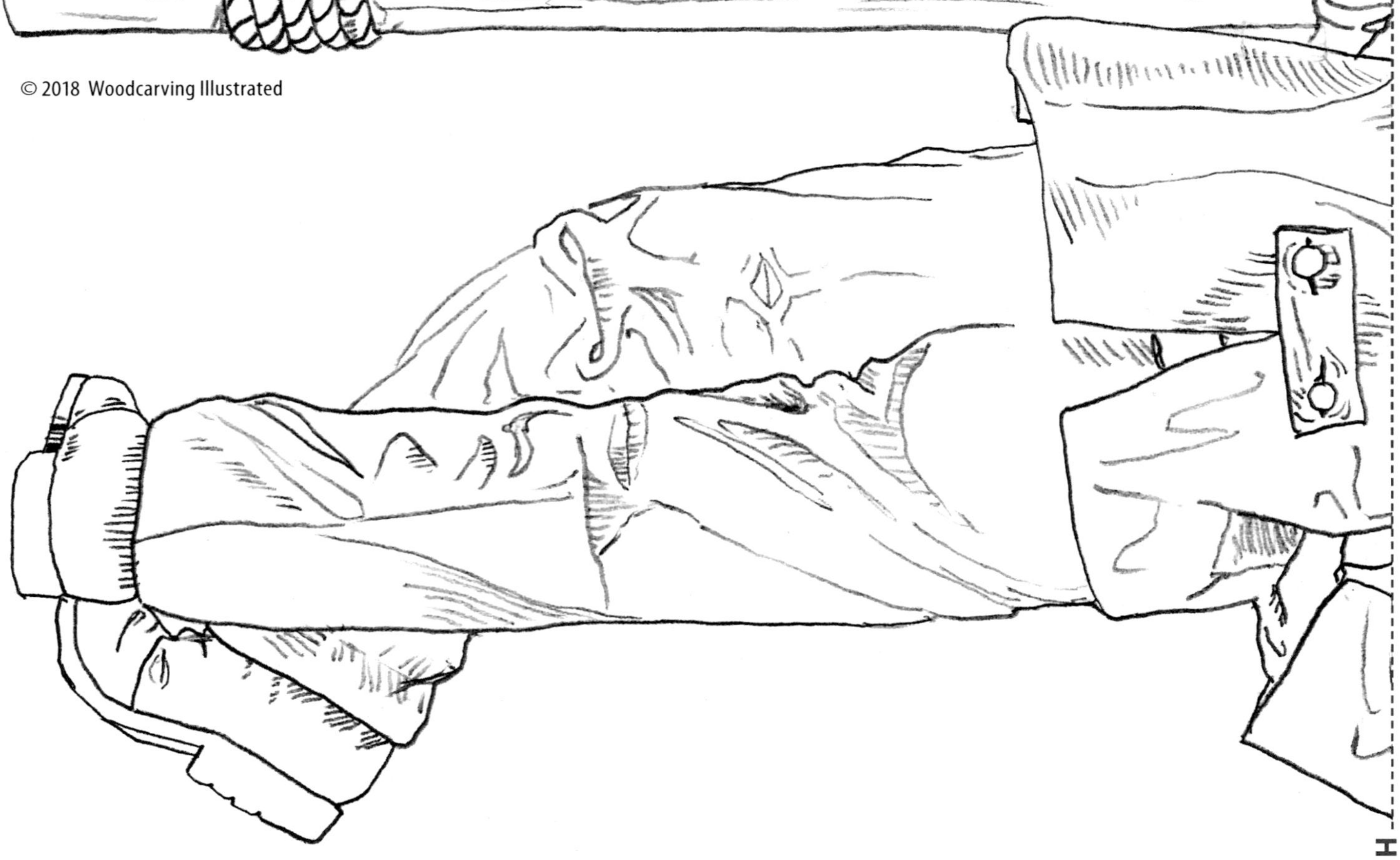
G
H